FRANCISCO INIESTA PÉREZ

RESOLUCIÓN DE PROBLEMAS EN LAS CLASES DE EDUCACIÓN FÍSICA

Título: RESOLUCIÓN DE PROBLEMAS EN LAS CLASES DE EDUCACIÓN FÍSICA

Autor: FRANCISCO INIESTA PÉREZ

Editorial: WANCEULEN EDITORIAL
Sello Editorial: WANCEULEN EDITORIAL DEPORTIVA

ISBN (Papel): 978-84-9993-958-2
ISBN (Ebook): 978-84-9993-959-9

DEPÓSITO LEGAL: SE 2356-2018

Impreso en España. 2018

WANCEULEN S.L.
C/ Cristo del Desamparo y Abandono, 56 - 41006 Sevilla
Dirección web: www.wanceuleneditorial.com y www.wanceulen.com
Email: info@wanceuleneditorial.com

ÍNDICE

INTRODUCCIÓN

En la **Introducción** del ***Decreto 54/2014,*** *por el que se establecen las enseñanzas mínimas y el currículo para Castilla-La Mancha correspondientes a la Educación Primaria*, en su anexo sobre Educación Física y que justifica este documento, expone que esta área tiene en el cuerpo y en la motricidad humana los elementos esenciales de su acción educativa y se orienta al desarrollo de las capacidades vinculadas a la actividad motriz y a la adquisición de elementos de cultura corporal que contribuyen al desarrollo personal y a una mejor calidad de vida.

La **E.F. en la etapa de Educación Primaria** tiene como finalidad principal desarrollar en el alumnado su competencia motriz, entendida como la integración de los conocimientos, procedimientos y actitudes que contribuyen a su desarrollo armónico e integral.

El **Real Decreto 126/2014,** se basa en la potenciación del aprendizaje por competencias, integradas en los elementos curriculares para propiciar una renovación en la práctica docente y en el proceso de enseñanza y aprendizaje. Como consecuencia de ello, la propuesta curricular del área de E.F. se ha organizado partiendo de las finalidades y criterios de evaluación que se persiguen y las competencias a desarrollar en la etapa.

Por otro lado, la **LOMCE** en **su Disposición adicional cuarta**, así como el **D.54/2014 en su artículo 2**, establecen que las administraciones educativas adoptarán medidas para que la actividad física y la dieta equilibrada formen parte del comportamiento infantil y juvenil, promoviendo la práctica diaria de deporte y ejercicio físico por parte de los alumnos y alumnas durante la jornada escolar.

En cuanto a la adopción de hábitos saludables, es importante tener en cuenta que hasta un 80% de niños y niñas en edad escolar únicamente participan en actividades físicas en la escuela, tal y como recoge el **Informe Eurydice, de la Comisión Europea (2013);** por ello, la Educación Física en estas edades debe tener una presencia importante en el horario del alumnado. El citado informe, siguiendo las pautas marcadas por la **Organización Mundial de la Salud**, aconseja para las edades escolares, 60 minutos diarios de actividad física.

Por tanto, debemos tener siempre en cuenta que una de las **finalidades principales de esta etapa escolar** es conseguir que los alumnos adopten hábitos de práctica continuada de actividad físico deportiva, higiene, y nutrición. Manifestación saludable a nivel físico y psíquico y de responsabilidad hacia uno mismo, los demás y el entorno, valorando los beneficios y perjuicios derivados del estilo de vida sana y cuidado del cuerpo.

Un reto al que se enfrentan los docentes de E.F. y los propios centros, es crear una verdadera **Escuela Activa**, donde la figura del maestro de E.F. promueve y guíe este proceso de cambio. Esta misión ha de realizarse de una manera coordinada e interrelacionada con el resto de la comunidad educativa, así como los agentes sociales responsables en la promoción de estilos de vida activos y saludables.

1. ANÁLISIS DEL PROBLEMA

El área de Educación Física presenta una problemática didáctica y metodológica muy diferente al resto de áreas que forman parte del currículum de Educación Primaria. Esto se debe a muy variados motivos, como son el espacio donde se desarrollan sus sesiones, la variedad de material que puede utilizarse, la diversidad de juegos y actividades que permiten el desarrollo de los contenidos y la consecución de los objetivos establecidos, la diversidad del alumnado presente en nuestras clases (a nivel físico, psicológico y social), la presencia de alumnado catalogado ACNEAE, etc.

Para intentar solucionar este aspecto y ayudar al resto de maestr@s y compañer@s de Educación Física, en el presente libro vamos a establecer una serie de casos prácticos donde se presenten diferentes problemáticas y sus posibles soluciones, si bien no son únicas, sí que pueden ser válidas si las aplicamos de manera adecuada.

Estos casos prácticos se encuentran adaptados a la normativa vigente LOE- LOMCE, no obstante, cada uno de ellos se concreta y contextualiza específicamente a la legislación de la Comunidad autónoma de Madrid o de Castilla-La Mancha.

El análisis de estos casos prácticos sigue unos pasos más o menos comunes, partiendo de una introducción y análisis de la situación, pasando por la contextualización del caso (población, centro, curso, nº de alumn@s...), haciendo referencia a la atención a la diversidad (ACNEAEs) y terminando con la intervención educativa (metodología, temporalización, recursos, interdisciplinariedad, elementos transversales, evaluación, desarrollo de sesiones...).

Cabe destacar que en este libro se analizan diferentes casos que se pueden dar en nuestros centros y en nuestras clases de Educación Física, todos ellos relacionados con contenidos curriculares (salud, esquema corporal, habilidades y destrezas motrices, actividades físicas en el medio natural, juegos y deportes, expresión corporal, etc.), no obstante aquí sólo vemos una "pequeñísima" parte de lo que nos podemos encontrar, ya que resultaría prácticamente imposible analizar y englobar toda la cantidad de casos y situaciones posibles, por lo que cada maestr@ dentro de su autonomía debe ser responsable de contextualizar estos casos a la problemática de su alumnado, de su centro, etc.

2 ERRORES MÁS COMUNES EN LA ELABORACIÓN DE UNIDADES DIDÁCTICAS Y/O SESIONES

A continuación, se describen algunos de los errores más frecuentes que cometemos los maestros de Educación Física a la hora de planificar y plantear nuestras Unidades Didácticas, nuestras sesiones e incluso nuestros juegos y actividades con nuestros alumnos y alumnas:

ERRORES POR LA UTILIZACIÓN DEL MATERIAL:

- **Demasiado material:** Se pretende demostrar que se sabe utilizar material variado, pero se suele caer en el error de trasladar demasiado material a las instalaciones o de cambiar continuamente de material, lo que provoca pérdida de tiempo. Sería válido en gimnasios donde el material no hay que trasladarlo o si utilizan varios alumnos-encargados para el transporte.
- **Cambio repetido de material:** Se utiliza un material que al cabo de unos ejercicios se recoge, se cambia por otro y luego se vuelve a utilizar.
- **Material inadecuado para la edad:** Se utiliza un material demasiado duro, peligroso o demasiado infantil.
- **Material inadecuado para las instalaciones:** Se utiliza material de gimnasio en el patio, o material de patio en sitios cerrados.
- **Utilización de muy poco material teniendo disponible** (según la actividad): Si en el almacén dispongo material suficiente para todos lo debo utilizar, por ejemplo, si tengo 8 balones utilizo los 8 para tener a más alumnos en actividad, y no sólo 2, 3, 4...

ERRORES EN LA PLANIFICACIÓN DE ACTIVIDADES:

- **Demasiadas actividades:** A menudo en la sesión se programan gran cantidad de actividades que no es posible llevar a cabo en el periodo de tiempo que dura la clase.
- **Pocas actividades:** Se realizan pocas actividades para que el alumno repita el ejercicio muchas veces, pero esto puede producir aburrimiento. Sí sería válido si las actividades son juegos que requieren mucho tiempo.

- **Actividades peligrosas:** Ejercicios que pueden provocar lesiones o caídas innecesarias.
- **Actividades que no se derivan de los objetivos programados o estándares de aprendizaje a evaluar:** Se pueden diseñar actividades muy bonitas, atractivas y motivantes, pero sin relación con los objetivos de la UD o de la sesión.
- **Actividades inadecuadas para los ACNEAEs:** Se programan actividades que algunos alumnos no pueden realizar por problemas de diverso tipo.

ERRORES EN LOS AGRUPAMIENTOS:

- **No se tiene en cuenta el número de alumnos/as:** Se programan actividades por parejas cuando los alumnos/as son impares, grupos de 4 alumnos/as cuando en el aula hay 22, estaciones que requieren 40 alumnos/as cuando solo hay 25...
- **Cambios repetidos:** Se cambia de forma sistemática de un tipo de agrupamiento a otro en cada actividad, provocando gran pérdida de tiempo.
- **Elección de equipos:** Se hacen agrupamientos, pero no se especifica la forma de elegirlos. Esto suele hacer perder el tiempo si no se tiene establecida la forma de agruparlos. Además, se suelen hacer discriminaciones por sexos y capacidades de los alumnos/as.

ERRORES EN LA ELECCIÓN DE LAS INSTALACIONES:

- **Instalaciones inadecuadas para los ejercicios:** Suelen hacerse sesiones en un gimnasio cuando las actividades que se realizan serían más apropiadas en espacios abiertos, o al contrario, realizar actividades propias de lugares cerrados en sitios abiertos. También el material influye a la hora de elegir uno u otro lugar.
- **Inadecuadas para el número de alumnos/as**: Hay veces en que se pretende llevar una sesión en una sala de usos múltiples de dimensiones reducidas con un número de alumnos/as demasiado grande. Sólo estaría justificado si los alumnos/as permanecen quietos durante bastante tiempo (ejercicios de relajación, estiramientos, representaciones grupales...).

3. FICHA SESIÓN

Cuando preparamos y desarrollamos una sesión de Educación Física debemos tener en cuenta y concretar una serie de elementos. A continuación, señalamos algunos de ellos:

- Nombre de la sesión
- Unidad didáctica a la que pertenece
- Nº de la sesión
- Curso a la que va dirigida
- Nº de alumnos
- Duración de la sesión
- Instalaciones
- Materiales a utilizar
- Objetivos didácticos o intenciones
- Contenidos a desarrollar
- Competencias que se pretenden conseguir
- Metodología y estilos metodológicos que se van a utilizar
- Estándares de aprendizaje que se van a evaluar, así como los instrumentos de evaluación que se van a utilizar.
- Partes de la sesión: inicial, principal y final
- Observaciones: papel del docente – atención a la diversidad
- Conclusión
- Bibliografía y webgrafía

4. CASOS PRÁCTICOS

CASO PRÁCTICO Nº1

Plantea una intervención didáctica divertida plasmada en una sesión con diferentes actividades y tareas para mejorar la lateralidad y la coordinación. Se debe tener en cuenta que el grupo-clase está formado por 21 alumno/as donde se encuentra un alumno con atrofia muscular.

1. INTRODUCCIÓN

El contenido de este supuesto es muy importante dentro de la E.F., pues trata aspectos fundamentales en nuestra área, pues una estructuración del esquema corporal es fundamental para la adquisición de aprendizajes básicos como la lectura y la escritura. Si bien es cierto, el contenido de este caso se desarrolla más ampliamente en el **tema 11** del temario de oposición de E.F., el cual trata sobre el esquema corporal y la lateralidad.

Como maestros de E.F., con el desarrollo de este supuesto intentaremos dotar a nuestro alumnado del mayor número de experiencias motrices posibles, aumentando su bagaje y competencia motriz, y, en definitiva, hacerlos más hábiles.

Por otro lado, para entender y comprender mejor el contenido de este caso comenzaremos con el análisis de una serie de conceptos que son inherentes al enunciado del mismo:

Sesión: Según **Pieron**, "es el punto de unión entre la programación, a veces muy teórica, y la realidad de la clase".

Unidad Didáctica: Jesús Viciana la define como "la unidad mínima del currículum del alumno con pleno sentido en sí misma, aunque contiene unidades más pequeñas que son las sesiones".

Esquema corporal: **Le Boulch** lo define como "la imagen o representación mental que tenemos de nuestro propio cuerpo".

Lateralidad: Según este mismo autor es "la predominancia motriz de los segmentos derechos o izquierdos del cuerpo"

ACNEAE (Decreto 66/2013): "Se considera ACNEAE todo aquel que recibe una respuesta educativa diferente a la ordinaria y que requiere determinados apoyos y provisiones educativas, por un periodo de escolarización o a lo largo de toda ella."

Hecha esta breve introducción pasaremos a analizar el segundo apartado de este supuesto.

2. MARCO LEGISLATIVO

La sesión que se nos pide, así como la U.D. en la que se enmarca, queda perfectamente justificada mediante la legislación vigente para el curso 2016/17 en nuestra comunidad de CLM a través de: **Ley Orgánica 8/2013 (LOMCE)**, **Ley Orgánica de Educación (LOE)**, la **Ley 7/2010, de Educación de Castilla-La Mancha**, el **Real Decreto 126/2014,** por el que se establece el **currículo básico de la Educación Primaria**, y más concretamente el **Decreto 54/2014,** por el que se establece **el currículo de la Educación Primaria en CLM.**

Además, tendremos en cuenta otra como:

- **D.66/2013** de atención a la diversidad en CLM
- **Orden 5/08/2014** de organización y evaluación de Primaria en CLM
- **Resolución 11/03/15** (categorización y ponderación de estándares)
- **Orden ECD65/2015** (relación de contenidos, criterios de evaluación y competencias)

Teniendo en cuenta este marco legislativo, pasaremos a contextualizar este supuesto práctico.

3. CONTEXTUALIZACIÓN

El centro en el que se desarrollará la sesión de este supuesto está situado en la comunidad de Castilla-La Mancha y cuenta con 499 alumnos. En relación con la E.F., el centro cuenta con un pabellón cubierto, dos pistas polideportivas al aire libre y una sala polivalente-multiusos cubierta.

Esta sesión se impartirá en el grupo **5ºA**, formado por **21 alumnos, 12 chicos y 11 chicas.** En general, el grupo es bastante participativo en las actividades de E.F.

Estos alumnos se encuentran en un intervalo de edad que oscila entre los 10 y los 11 años. Algunas de sus características psicoevolutivas más destacadas son:

- **A nivel cognitivo:** Se sitúan en el estadio de las operaciones formales de Piaget, lo que les permite realizar operaciones mentales abstractas.

- **A nivel socio-afectivo:** Empiezan progresivamente a independizarse de los adultos, aumentando su autonomía y afianzando su personalidad.

- **A nivel motriz:** Comienzan los procesos característicos de la pubertad (crecimiento, aumento de musculatura, etc.). Consolidad su esquema corporal y toman conciencia global de su cuerpo, sistematizan hábitos higiénicos y respetan las medidas de seguridad.

Dentro del grupo encontramos **un alumno** con atrofia muscular por desuso, por falta de actividad en sus extremidades superiores debido a un grave accidente que le ha obligado a tener sus dos brazos escayolados. Este alumno participará con sus compañeros en todas las actividades y se le adaptarán los ejercicios y los materiales (peso, tamaño...) cuando por falta de fuerza no pueda utilizarlo. Así mismo, se les da a él y a la familia recomendaciones de ejercicios de fortalecimiento para recuperar el tono muscular.

Una vez analizado el contexto, pasaremos a analizar la intervención educativa del supuesto que se nos pide.

4. INTERVENCIÓN EDUCATIVA

4.1. RELACIÓN CON EL CURRÍCULUM

Con el trabajo de esta sesión contribuiremos a conseguir **diversos elementos curriculares** marcados en el **D.54/2014**, tales como el **Objetivo de Etapa "k"**: "*"Valorar la higiene y la salud, aceptar el propio cuerpo y el de los otros, respetar las diferencias y utilizar la educación física y el deporte como medios para favorecer el desarrollo personal y social"*. Así como las **Competencias Clave "Sociales y Cívicas" o "Aprender a Aprender"** a través de las interacciones que se dan en los juegos y actividades.

También podemos destacar el Bloque de Contenidos nº1 que se trabaja en todos los cursos de Primaria "Actividad física y salud", con contenidos como "Fijación de la lateralidad", "Dominio corporal" o "Segmentos corporales".

Así mismo, el contenido de la sesión lo evaluaremos con el **Criterio de Evaluación nº1** para 5º de Primaria: "Utiliza nuevas habilidades motrices o combinaciones de las mismas**...",** y su **estándar de aprendizaje evaluable 1.3.**: "Adapta las habilidades motrices básicas de manipulación de objetos a diferentes tipos de entornos y actividades".

Por último, no nos podemos olvidar el **Decreto 66/2013** que regula la respuesta a la diversidad educativa en CLM, o el **Decreto 3/2008** de convivencia escolar en CLM.

4.2. METODOLOGÍA

En nuestra labor docente y a la hora de poner en práctica nuestra sesión, deberemos tener en cuenta lo marcado en el **D.54/**2014 y procurar que el aprendizaje de nuestros alumnos/as sea significativo, con un carácter lúdico y global, mediante una enseñanza individualizada y atendiendo a la diversidad del alumnado.

Así mismo, también tendremos en cuenta lo establecido en la **Orden 65/2015 en su anexo II** que establece orientaciones metodológicas para el trabajo por competencias en el aula y recomienda utilizar metodologías activas como del aprendizaje cooperativo, el aprendizaje por proyectos o el aprendizaje basado en problemas.

En este sentido, los **estilos de enseñanza** que utilizaremos serán fundamentalmente la resolución de problemas, el descubrimiento guiado y la asignación de tareas. Trabajaremos diversos tipos de **agrupamientos** y las **instalaciones y materiales** a utilizar vendrán condicionados por las actividades y objetivos a conseguir.

4.3. TEMPORALIZACIÓN Y RECURSOS

Esta sesión se enmarca dentro de la **UD número 10** de nuestra programación y se titula **"Me gustan los alternativos",** la cual consta de **8 sesiones,** de las cuales desarrollaremos la **número 7.** Esta U.D. se desarrolla en el **tercer trimestre** y su secuenciación es la siguiente:

- Sesión 1: ¿Conoces los alternativos?
- Sesión 2: Jugamos con las indiacas
- Sesión 3: Pásame la indiaca
- Sesión 4: ¿Es un disco o es un plato?
- Sesión 5: ¿Qué hacemos con los sticks?
- Sesión 6: Vamos a palear
- Sesión 7: El circuito alternativo
- Sesión 8: ¿Controlas los alternativos?

4.4. INTERDISCIPLINARIEDAD Y ELEMENTOS TRANSVERSALES

A través de esta sesión se puede plantear un trabajo interdisciplinar con otras áreas, por ejemplo, con el área de lengua mediante la realización de fichas sobre material alternativo, o la construcción del mismo desde el área de Educación Artística.

Además, esta sesión se encuentra estrechamente relacionada con el **proyecto deportivo** que desarrolla nuestro centro *"El colegio se mueve"*, en el cual participa todo el claustro, con actividades como "Los recreos deportivos" o "los desayunos saludables".

Por otro lado, siguiendo el **RD 126/2014,** a través de esta sesión trabajamos una serie de contenidos que pueden ser trabajados desde todas las áreas, conocidos como **elementos transversales,** como por ejemplo Educación Cívica o Educación para la actividad física y la dieta equilibrada.

4.5. EVALUACIÓN

Según la **Orden 5/08/2014** y lo establecido en nuestra programación, la **evaluación de nuestro alumnado será continua**, siendo evaluados en todas las sesiones a través de diferentes estándares de aprendizaje evaluables.

Para valorar la consecución de estos estándares se utilizarán diferentes **instrumentos de evaluación** como el registro anecdotario, las listas de control o una rúbrica. Además, utilizaremos la herramienta evaluativa **"Evalúa 2.00",** la cual, siguiendo la **Resolución 11/03/15,** categoriza los estándares en: Básicos (50%), Intermedios (40%) y Avanzados (10%), en nuestro centro.

Cabe destacar que la evaluación se llevará a cabo tanto con los alumnos, como con el proceso de enseñanza y la propia práctica docente.

4.6. DESARROLLO DE LA SESIÓN

Hecho este breve análisis del supuesto, pasaremos a desarrollar la sesión que se nos pide, la cual se desarrollará fundamentalmente a través de un circuito de 6 postas durante la parte principal.

En primer lugar, analizaremos algunos aspectos a tener en cuenta:

Duración: 1 hora

Instalación: Pista polideportiva

Material: Indiacas, discos voladores, palas...

Contenidos: El juego y el deporte como fenómenos sociales. Deportes alternativos. Aceptación y respeto a las normas. Valoración del esfuerzo personal. Habilidades motrices. Lateralidad.

Metodología: Asignación de tareas, resolución de problemas...

Competencias Clave: Competencias Sociales y Cívicas, Aprender a Aprender

Objetivos didácticos:

- Trabajar/Jugar cooperativamente con los compañeros.

- Respetar las normas, el material y los compañeros.

- Adoptar hábitos higiénicos básicos y saludables.

Evaluación: Estándares de aprendizaje evaluables:

- 1.4.1. Respeta la diversidad de realidades corporales y de niveles de competencia motriz.

- 2.1.3. Adapta las habilidades motrices básicas de manipulación de objetos

- 1.8.2. Demuestra autonomía y confianza en diferentes situaciones

- 1.8.4. Participa en la recogida y organización del material

- 1.8.5. Acepta formar parte del grupo y el resultado de las competiciones con deportividad

Hecho este análisis de la sesión, a continuación, pasaremos a su desarrollo, el cual dividiremos en 3 partes:

1ª PARTE: ANIMACIÓN (Y CALENTAMIENTO) (10'-15')

En primer lugar, nos dirigiremos al aula de los alumnos, donde pasaremos lista, revisaremos que traen el material adecuado (chándal y bolsa de aseo) y se nombran los encargados, explicaremos brevemente el contenido de la sesión. Después los alumnos/as se colocan en fila y se dirigen en orden hacia la pista polideportiva, colocan sus bolsas de aseo y se sientan en el centro de la pista a esperar las indicaciones del profesor. Cuando estén todos sentados y en silencio explicaremos el primer juego, el cual servirá de calentamiento.

- Juego: "Haz lo que yo digo": El maestro irá indicando una serie de acciones que los alumnos/as deberán realizar, por ejemplo: tocar una canasta, una portería, subir y bajar las escaleras del patio, desplazarse en cuadrupedia, hacer grupos de 3, de 4, de 6... La última indicación será hacer grupos de 4, que nos servirán para la parte principal.

2ª PARTE: PARTE PRINCIPAL (~30'-35')

En esta parte realizaremos un circuito dividido en 6 postas. Cada grupo se ubicará en una posta tras la explicación del maestro. En cada posta estaremos 6-7 minutos y, a la señal de cambio, éste se realizará en el sentido de las agujas del reloj. Antes de cambiar de estación se debe dejar el material ordenado dentro de un aro.

Las estaciones del circuito son:

1. Indiacas: Pases, golpeos, recepciones...
2. Palas de madera: golpeos individuales, por parejas...
3. Discos voladores: Pases, recepciones...
4. Pelota gigante: Pases, recepciones...
5. Floorball: Zig-zag entre conos, minigolf...
6. Bolos

3ª PARTE: PARTE FINAL Y VUELTA A LA CALMA (5'-10')

Terminamos la sesión con la recogida y almacenamiento del material por parte de los alumno/as. Posteriormente los alumnos/as cogerán sus bolsas de aseo e irán al aseo a cumplir el objetivo higiénico. Por último, volverán a su aula en fila y en silencio.

NOTAS ACLARATORIAS A LA SESIÓN:

El maestro deberá estar pendiente de que el alumno con atrofia muscular no presenta ningún problema para realizar las actividades. Si fuese necesario le podría ayudar con la utilización de algunos materiales o adaptación de los mismos.

CASO PRÁCTICO Nº 2

Queremos plantear una sesión que sea evaluada con el estándar de aprendizaje para 5º de Educación Primaria 2.4. "Construye composiciones grupales en interacción con los compañeros utilizando los recursos expresivos del cuerpo y partiendo de estímulos musicales, plásticos o verbales".

En dicha clase de 5º encontramos un alumno introvertido y poco aceptado por los compañeros, por lo que su socialización con ellos es muy baja.

1. INTRODUCCIÓN

El contenido de esta situación práctica es muy importante dentro de la E.F., pues trata aspectos fundamentales en nuestra área como **las habilidades expresivas,** aspectos que se desarrollan más ampliamente en el **tema 12** del temario de oposición de E.F.

Las habilidades expresivas son de carácter innato y natural en el hombre, por lo que al igual que desarrollamos el resto de habilidades y capacidades del individuo, también deben educarse y desarrollarse en la escuela, por lo que será uno de nuestros objetivos fundamentales en este supuesto: hacer al alumno/a más competente en el uso de las habilidades expresivas.

Por otro lado, para entender y comprender mejor el contenido de este problema comenzaremos con el análisis de una serie de conceptos que son inherentes al enunciado del mismo:

Sesión: Según **Pieron**, "es el punto de unión entre la programación, a veces muy teórica, y la realidad de la clase".

Unidad Didáctica: **Jesús Viciana** la define como "la unidad mínima del currículum del alumno con pleno sentido en sí misma, aunque contiene unidades más pequeñas que son las sesiones".

Expresión corporal: Según **Paloma de Santiago** "es el lenguaje del cuerpo, el lenguaje natural del hombre, el más inmediato y propio de él".

Estándar de aprendizaje: Según el RD 126/14 en su artículo 2, "son especificaciones de los criterios de evaluación y permiten entender el resultado del aprendizaje, y concretan lo que el alumno debe saber, comprender y saber hacer en cada asignatura".

2. MARCO LEGISLATIVO

La sesión que se nos pide, así como la U.D. en la que se enmarca, queda perfectamente justificada mediante la legislación vigente para el curso 2016/17 en nuestra comunidad de CLM a través de: **Ley Orgánica 8/2013 (LOMCE)**, **Ley Orgánica de Educación (LOE)**, el **Real Decreto 126/2014,** por el que se establece el **currículo básico de la Educación Primaria a nivel nacional**, y más concretamente el **Decreto 89/2014,** por el que se establece **el currículo de la Educación Primaria en la Comunidad de Madrid.**

Además, tendremos en cuenta otra como:

Orden ECD65/2015 (relación de contenidos, criterios de evaluación y competencias)

Decreto 15/2007, por el que se establece el marco regulador de la convivencia en los centros docentes de la Comunidad de Madrid.

Orden 3622/2014, por la que se regulan determinados aspectos de organización y funcionamiento, así como la evaluación y los documentos de aplicación en la Educación Primaria

- ***Orden 11994/2012,*** *por la que se regula la jornada escolar en los centros docentes*
- **LEY 2/2010,** de **Autoridad del Profesor**.

Teniendo en cuenta este marco legislativo, pasaremos a contextualizar esta situación.

3. CONTEXTUALIZACIÓN

El centro en el que se desarrollará la sesión está situado en la **Comunidad de Madrid** y cuenta con **499 alumnos**, además **el centro cuenta con jornada continuada de 9 a 14 horas**. Esta sesión/UD se impartirá en el grupo **5ºA**, formado por **25 alumnos, 14 chicos y 11 chicas.** En general, el grupo es bastante participativo en las actividades de E.F.

Cabe destacar que dentro del grupo encontramos un **alumno** con unas características especiales, concretamente es muy **introvertido y poco aceptado** en clase por los compañeros. En esta sesión nos centraremos en que tenga una mejor integración en el grupo y aumente la participación y motivación en las diferentes actividades expresivas. Intentaremos contribuir a ello también a través del **Programa Deportivo** de nuestro centro ("Nuestro colegio se mueve") con las actividades que se realizan tanto en horario escolar como en horario extraescolar (recreos activos, representaciones, bailes de convivencia, bailes de navidad, etc.).

Por otro lado, los alumnos de 5º de Primaria se encuentran en un intervalo de edad que oscila entre los **10 y los 11 años.** Algunas de sus **características psicoevolutivas** más destacadas son: (poner las del curso que nos pidan, por ejemplo:

A nivel cognitivo: Se sitúan en el estadio de las operaciones formales de Piaget, lo que les permite realizar operaciones mentales abstractas.

A nivel socio-afectivo: Empiezan progresivamente a independizarse de los adultos, aumentando su autonomía y afianzando su personalidad.

A nivel motriz: Comienzan los procesos característicos de la pubertad (crecimiento, aumento de musculatura, etc.). Consolidad su esquema corporal y toman conciencia global de su cuerpo, sistematizan hábitos higiénicos y respetan las medidas de seguridad.

Una vez analizado el contexto, pasaremos a analizar la intervención educativa.

4. INTERVENCIÓN EDUCATIVA

4.1. RELACIÓN CON EL CURRÍCULUM

Con el trabajo de esta sesión contribuiremos a conseguir **diversos elementos curriculares** marcados en el **D.89/2014**, tales como el **Objetivo/s de Etapa "k":** Valorar la higiene y la salud, conocer y respetar el cuerpo humano, y utilizar la educación física y el deporte como medios para favorecer el desarrollo personal y social, o el **"j":** **"**Utilizar diferentes representaciones y expresiones artísticas e iniciarse en la construcción". Así como las **Competencias Sociales y cívicas,** mediante las interacciones sociales que se dan en los juegos y actividades **o conciencia y expresiones culturales** a través a través de la expresión de ideas o sentimientos de forma creativa y de la práctica de bailes y danzas populares**, entre otras.**

También podemos destacar los **contenidos: "Desarrollo de las habilidades corporales artístico-expresivas en forma individual o en grupo" o "La danza".** Así como el **Criterio de Evaluación nº2**: "Utilizar los recursos expresivos del cuerpo y el movimiento, de forma estética y creativa, comunicando sensaciones, emociones e ideas.**"**, y los **estándares de aprendizaje evaluables: 2.1. "**Representa personajes, situaciones, ideas y sentimientos utilizando los recursos expresivos del cuerpo individualmente, en parejas o en grupos**" o el 2.4.** "Construye composiciones grupales en interacción con los compañeros utilizando los recursos expresivos del cuerpo y partiendo de estímulos musicales, plásticos o verbales".

4.2. METODOLOGÍA

En nuestra labor docente y a la hora de poner en práctica nuestra sesión, deberemos procurar que el aprendizaje de nuestros alumnos/as sea significativo, con un carácter lúdico y global, mediante una enseñanza individualizada y atendiendo a la diversidad del alumnado.

En este sentido, podemos destacar algunas de las **Orientaciones metodológicas** que se citan **en la Introducción del Anexo de E.F. del D89/2014, por ejemplo, favorecer el trabajo libre, usar una práctica y progresiva en la actividad, dosificando el esfuerzo desde actividades más cortas y frecuentes hasta las de mayor duración y aprovechar las posibilidades del lenguaje corporal favoreciendo actividades como la danza y, en general, las de expresión corporal.**

Así mismo, también tendremos en cuenta lo establecido en la **Orden 65/2015 en su anexo II** que establece orientaciones metodológicas para el trabajo por competencias en el aula y recomienca utilizar metodologías activas como del aprendizaje cooperativo, el aprendizaje por proyectos o el aprendizaje basado en problemas.

En cuanto a los **estilos de enseñanza** cue utilizaremos serán fundamentalmente la resolución de problemas, el descubrimiento guiado y la asignación de tareas. Trabajaremos diversos tipos de **agrupamientos** y las **instalaciones y materiales** serán los propios del área y los que puedan aportar los alumnos/as.

4.3. TEMPORALIZACIÓN Y RECURSOS

Esta sesión se enmarca dentro de la **UD número 5** de nuestra programación y se titula **"Somos artistas",** la cual consta de **8 sesiones** que se desarrolla en el **primer trimestre**.

La secuenciación de estas sesiones es la siguiente:

- **Sesión 1: "QUE EMPIECE EL ESPECTÁCULO"**
- **Sesión 2: "CUENTAME UN CUENTO"**
- **Sesión 3: "A HACER EL MIMO"**
- **Sesión 4: "VAMOS A BAILAR"**
- **Sesión 5: "BAILA BAILA"**
- **Sesión 6: "LAS SITUACIONES DIVERTIDAS"**
- **Sesión 7: "SEGUIMOS ENSAYANDO"**

- **Sesión 8: "LUCES, CÁMARA, ¡¡ACCIÓN!!"**

A continuación, desarrollaremos la **sesión nº 7: "Seguimos ensayando".**

En relación con los **recursos** de nuestro centro relacionados con la E.F. y con el supuesto que nos ocupa, el centro cuenta con un pabellón cubierto y una sala polivalente-multiusos cubierta, los cuales cumplen con la normativa establecida en el **RD 132/2010.**

En cuanto al **material,** nuestra área cuenta con el material suficiente y necesario para impartir correctamente las sesiones de esta U.D., por ejemplo: aros, cuerdas, telas, etc. Así como el material propio de los alumnos: zapatillas, ropa deportiva, bosa de aseo; y del maestro para la gestión, organización y control de la clase.

También destacamos el **uso de las TIC** en las sesiones de esta U.D., por ejemplo: el uso del proyector y la pantalla digital para el visionado de videos de diferentes bailes, los Netbook de los alumnos/as para la realización de un trabajo de investigación...

4.4. INTERDISCIPLINARIEDAD Y ELEMENTOS TRANSVERSALES

A través de esta sesión se puede plantear un **trabajo interdisciplinar** con otras áreas como **Lengua** a través de la realización de trabajos de investigación o los diálogos que se producen en las representaciones de cada grupo, o con la de **Educación Artística** mediante la práctica de bailes y la realización de disfraces, decoración, etc.

Además, esta sesión se encuentra estrechamente relacionada con el **PROGRAMA DEPORTIVO** que desarrolla nuestro centro *"El colegio se mueve"* con actividades como "El Taller de teatro, Los bailes solidarios, Festival y bailes de Navidad, etc.

Por otro lado, siguiendo el **DECRETO 89/2014 (artículo 8),** a través de esta sesión trabajamos una serie de contenidos que pueden ser trabajados desde todas las áreas, conocidos como **elementos transversales,** como por ejemplo Educación para la comprensión lectora y hábito de lectura, expresión oral y escrita, Educación para la igualdad efectiva entre hombres y mujeres o Educación para la actividad física y la dieta equilibrada.

4.5. EVALUACIÓN

Según la **Orden 3622/2014**, y lo establecido en nuestra programación, la **evaluación de nuestro alumnado será continua y global**, siendo evaluados en todas las sesiones a través de diferentes estándares de aprendizaje evaluables.

Para valorar la consecución de estos estándares se utilizarán diferentes **instrumentos de evaluación** como el registro anecdotario, las listas de control o rúbricas.

También cabe destacar que la evaluación se llevará a cabo tanto con los alumnos, como con el proceso de enseñanza y la propia práctica docente.

4.6. ATENCIÓN A LA DIVERSIDAD

Para atender correctamente a todo el alumnado seguiremos lo marcado en la normativa que regula la atención personalizada del alumnado en nuestra comunidad a través de la ***Orden 1493/2015,*** destacando la **coordinación** necesaria con el equipo de orientación, jefatura de estudios, tutor, familias...

4.7. DESARROLLO DE LA SESIÓN

Como hemos comentado anteriormente vamos a desarrollar la sesión número 7 de la unidad didáctica relacionada con la expresión corporal. Durante esta sesión los alumnos/as se dedicarán principalmente a continuar con los ensayos de las propuestas escénicas que se establecieron en la sesión anterior.

La temática de las representaciones es "Los anuncios publicitarios". Los alumnos/as se dividieron en 5 grupos de 5 alumnos/as cada uno. Estos grupos se formaron al azar, la mayoría por afinidad, salvo el alumno introvertido que fue asignado en el grupo de 4 compañeros/as con los que tiene "mejor" relación, a los cuales no les importó que formara parte de su grupo.

Las instrucciones que se les dio a cada grupo es que deberían realizar un anuncio televisivo en el que anunciaran un invento original, algo que no exista y que fuese de gran ayuda para la humanidad. Así mismo se les permitió utilizar los materiales propios de EF y aquellos que ellos mismos pudieran aportar (pañuelos, trapos, periódicos, cartones...).

Hecho este breve análisis del contenido de la sesión, pasaremos analizar algunos aspectos a tener en cuenta:

- **Título**: "Seguimos ensayando"
- **Curso**: 5ºA
- **Nº de alumnos**: 25, 14 chicos y 11 chicas
- **Duración**: 1 hora
- **Instalación**: Sala polivalente
- **Material**: Los propios de EF y los aportados por los alumnos/as
- **Contenidos:** Representar personajes, situaciones, ideas y sentimientos. Expresar movimientos a partir de estímulos rítmicos o musicales. Exponer ideas de forma coherente. Uso correcto de materiales y espacios. Aceptación y respeto hacia las normas, reglas, estrategias y personas que participan en el juego.
- **Objetivos didácticos**:

- Conocer e interiorizar la posición y el control del cuerpo, en posturas poco habituales, así como en desplazamientos que impliquen la totalidad del cuerpo.

- Utilizar de manera correcta los espacios y materiales.

- Promover la participación, la desinhibición personal y la compenetración grupal.

- Manifestar solidaridad y compañerismo en cualquier actividad física, aceptando y colaborando con todos los compañeros sin distinción.

- Reconocer sensaciones, ideas y estados de ánimo en otros compañeros, a través del gesto y del movimiento.

- **Metodología:** Descubrimiento guiado, resolución de problemas
- **Competencias Clave**: Competencias Sociales y Cívicas, Conciencia y expresiones culturales
- **Evaluación:**

- **Instrumentos de evaluación:** Registro anecdotario, lista de control, rúbrica

- **Estándares de aprendizaje:**

2.1. Representa personajes, situaciones, ideas y sentimientos utilizando los recursos expresivos del cuerpo individualmente, en parejas o en grupos.

2.2. Representa o expresa movimientos a partir de estímulos rítmicos o musicales, individualmente, en parejas o grupos.

2.4. Construye composiciones grupales en interacción con los compañeros utilizando los recursos expresivos del cuerpo y partiendo de estímulos musicales, plásticos o verbales.

12.3. Expone sus ideas de forma coherente y se expresa de forma correcta en diferentes situaciones y respeta las opiniones de los demás.

13.3. Incorpora en sus rutinas el cuidado e higiene del cuerpo.

13.4. Participa en la recogida y organización de material utilizado en las clases.

13.5. Acepta formar parte del grupo que le corresponda y el resultado de las competiciones con deportividad.

Hecho este análisis de la sesión, a continuación, pasaremos a su desarrollo, el cual dividiremos en 3 partes:

1ª PARTE: ANIMACIÓN (10'-15')

En primer lugar, nos dirigiremos al aula de los alumnos, donde pasaremos lista, revisaremos que traen el material adecuado (chándal y bolsa de aseo) y se nombran los encargados, explicaremos brevemente el contenido de la sesión. Después los alumnos/as se colocan en fila y se dirigen en orden hacia la sala polivalente, entran y colocan sus bolsas de aseo sobre un banco y se sientan en el centro a esperar las indicaciones del maestro. Cuando estén todos sentados y en silencio explicaremos el primer juego, el cual servirá para desinhibir a los alumnos y donde el maestro participará como uno más, centrándose en el alumno introvertido para motivarlo (lo utilizará a modo de ejemplo en las demostraciones).

- Juego: "Los saludos": Todos los alumnos/as se mueven libremente por todo el espacio y, siguiendo las órdenes del maestro, se saludaran de diferentes formas con el resto de sus compañeros:

- Saludo formal chocando la mano

- Chocar la mano en el aire

- Con un abrazo

- Con un beso

- Con saludos inventados

- Etc.

Para seguir con la dinámica de los saludos, a continuación, trabajaremos los diferentes tipos de abrazo: abrazo del oso, abrazo del pulpo, abrazo del koala, abrazo del topo, abrazo del canguro, etc.

2ª PARTE: PARTE PRINCIPAL (~30'-35')

Esta parte de la sesión la dividiremos en 2 partes:

- En una primera parte ensayaremos durante 10-15 minutos el baile que se propuso para realizar en el "Festival de Navidad", el cual los alumnos/as ya aprendieron en sesiones anteriores.
- En la segunda parte, durante 15-20 minutos, los alumnos/as se organizarán en los grupos establecidos en la sesión nº6 y ensayaran "los anuncios publicitarios". Estos anuncios se representarán en la sesión nº8 y en ella los alumnos/as serán evaluados por sus propios compañeros (coevaluación).

En esta segunda parte el maestro se dedicará a pasar por todos los grupos concretando ideas, motivando y ayudando a la organización y puesta en escena de la representación.

3ª PARTE: PARTE FINAL (5'-10')

Terminamos la sesión con la recogida y almacenamiento del material por parte de los alumno/as. Posteriormente los alumnos/as cogerán sus bolsas de aseo e irán al aseo a cumplir el objetivo higiénico. Por último, volverán a su aula en fila y en silencio.

Durante esta última parte aprovecharemos para realizar algunas reflexiones finales sobre la sesión, realizar las anotaciones pertinentes en nuestro cuaderno y anticipar el contenido de la próxima sesión (para motivar).

CASO PRÁCTICO Nº 3

Vamos a celebrar una jornada de convivencia para grupos de 4º, 5º y 6º de primaria en un centro de doble línea (6 grupos en total) en un parque periurbano cercano al centro, concretamente a 2 km. Se debe tener en cuenta la presencia de los siguientes alumnos:

Un alumno en silla de ruedas.

Dos alumn@s con retraso mental.

Un alumno con esguince y muletas.

1. INTRODUCCIÓN

El contenido de este supuesto es muy importante dentro de la E.F., pues trata sobre una de las prioridades que todos los centros educativos de nuestra comunidad deben incluir en su P.G.A. como es la realización de actividades deportivas incluidas dentro de un **proyecto deportivo** con el objetivo de mejorar la salud y la calidad de vida de nuestro alumnado.

Las actividades que vamos a desarrollar en esta jornada de convivencia son tratadas en diversos temas dentro del temario para las oposiciones, pero especialmente el **tema 15:** "La Educación Física y el deporte como elemento sociocultural. Juegos y deportes populares, autóctonos y tradicionales. Las actividades físicas organizadas en el medio natural".

Hoy en día, nadie discute que la actividad física y deportiva es uno de los grandes pilares para tener una buena salud. Además de conseguir que nuestros alumn@s realicen más actividades físicas, uno de los grandes objetivos que nos planteamos como especialistas es transmitir y promocionar en su práctica unos valores de convivencia, deportividad, tolerancia, igualdad, juego limpio..., además de enseñarles a realizarlas de forma correcta (calentamientos previos, vestimenta apropiada, higiene personal, nutrición adecuada...).

Por otro lado, para comprender mejor el contenido de este supuesto analizaremos una serie de conceptos que se encuentran estrechamente relacionados con el enunciado del mismo.

En primer lugar, la **PGA** es un documento propio y específico de cada centro educativo donde se recogen los objetivos que se persiguen en el curso actual, así como las medidas o acciones para conseguirlos.

También debemos destacar el concepto de **Programa o Proyecto Deportivo Escolar,** el cual se define como el conjunto de actividades físicas y deportivas que se realizan en el centro educativo, en horario lectivo y no lectivo, con el fin de promover e inculcar un estilo de vida saludable a través del deporte.

Por último, el concepto alrededor del cual gira todo el supuesto es el de **salud,** que la **OMS y Terris** definen como "el estado de completo bienestar físico, mental y social, y no solamente la ausencia de afecciones o invalideces".

Otros conceptos a tener en cuenta son:

- **Recreación**: *"Es una actividad que saca al individuo de su vida cotidiana lo divierte, entretiene y distrae"* (***Jorge Guajardo***).

- **Juegos populares**: *"Actividades lúdicas de carácter local y ancestral que provienen de la presión de generaciones anteriores y que poseen enmarcado carácter cultural desde un punto de vista antropológico"* (***Cristóbal Moreno Palos***).

- **Orientación**: *"Deporte donde los competidores completan un recorrido navegando entre unos controles de paso que vienen marcados sobre un mapa"* (***Federación Internacional de Orientación***).

- **Convivencia**: Según el diccionario de la Real Academia Española es *"la acción de vivir en compañía de otro u otros"*.

- **ACNEAE (Decreto 89/2014, artículo 17):** "Se considera ACNEAE todo aquellos alumnos que requieran una atención educativa diferente a la ordinaria por presentar necesidades educativas especiales por discapacidad, por dificultades específicas de aprendizaje (entre ellas la dislexia), por presentar Trastorno por Déficit de Atención e Hiperactividad (TDAH), por sus altas capacidades intelectuales, por su incorporación tardía al sistema educativo, o por condiciones personales o de historia escolar." (Sólo si el supuesto presenta un ACNEAE).

Hecha esta breve introducción pasaremos a analizar el segundo apartado de este supuesto.

2. MARCO LEGISLATIVO

La sesión que se nos pide, así como la U.D. en la que se enmarca, queda perfectamente justificada mediante la legislación vigente para el curso 2016/17 en nuestra comunidad de Madrid a través de: **Ley Orgánica 8/2013 (LOMCE)**, **Ley Orgánica de Educación (LOE)**, el **Real Decreto 126/2014,** por el que se establece el **currículo básico de la Educación Primaria a nivel**

nacional, y más concretamente el **Decreto 89/2014,** por el que se establece **el currículo de la Educación Primaria en la Comunidad de Madrid.**

Además, tendremos en cuenta otra como:

- **Orden ECD65/2015** (relación de contenidos, criterios de evaluación y competencias)

- **ORDEN 1493/2015,** por la que se regula la evaluación y la promoción de los alumnos con necesidad específica de apoyo educativo

- **Orden 3622/2014,** por la que se regulan determinados aspectos de organización y funcionamiento, así como la evaluación y los documentos de aplicación en la Educación Primaria

- **Decreto 15/2007,** por el que se establece el marco regulador de la convivencia en los centros docentes de la Comunidad *de Madrid.*

- **LEY 2/2010,** de **Autoridad del Profesor**.

Teniendo en cuenta este marco legislativo, pasaremos a contextualizar este supuesto práctico.

3. CONTEXTUALIZACIÓN

El centro en el que se desarrollará la sesión está situado en la **Comunidad de Madrid** y cuenta con **313 alumnos**, además **el centro cuenta con jornada continuada de 9 a 14 horas**. El total de alumnos a los que va destinada la jornada son **165**, de los cursos **4º, 5º y 6º**.

Estos alumnos se encuentran en un intervalo de edad que oscila entre los 9 y 12 años. Algunas de sus **características psicoevolutivas** más destacadas son:

A nivel cognitivo: Se sitúan en el estadio de las operaciones formales de Piaget, lo que les permite realizar operaciones mentales abstractas.

A nivel socio-afectivo: Empiezan progresivamente a independizarse de los adultos, aumentando su autonomía y afianzando su personalidad.

A nivel motriz: Comienzan los procesos característicos de la pubertad (crecimiento, aumento de musculatura, etc.). Consolidad su esquema corporal y toman conciencia global de su cuerpo, sistematizan hábitos higiénicos y respetan las medidas de seguridad.

Entre estos alumnos/as encontramos **cuatro que presentan unas características especiales** que deberemos tener en cuenta, que serán concretados en el apartado de atención a la diversidad.

Una vez analizado el contexto, pasaremos a analizar la intervención educativa del supuesto que se nos pide.

4. INTERVENCIÓN EDUCATIVA

4.1. RELACIÓN CON EL CURRÍCULUM

En primer lugar, podemos destacar que la **LOMCE en su Disposición adicional cuarta** señala que: "Las administraciones educativas adoptarán medidas para que la **actividad física** y la **dieta equilibrada** formen parte del comportamiento infantil y juvenil. A estos efectos, promoverán la práctica diaria de **deporte y ejercicio** durante la jornada escolar...". De aquí se desprende la justificación o necesidad de elaboración de los proyectos deportivos en los centros escolares.

Por otro lado, con el trabajo de esta sesión contribuiremos a conseguir **diversos elementos curriculares** marcados en el **D.89/2014**, tales como los **Objetivos de Etapa "k":** Valorar la higiene y la salud, conocer y respetar el cuerpo humano, y utilizar la educación física y el deporte como medios para favorecer el desarrollo personal y social", "**m**": "*Desarrollar las capacidades afectivas en todos los ámbitos de la personalidad y en sus relaciones con los demás así como una actitud contraria a la violencia, a los perjuicios de cualquier tipo y a los estereotipos sexistas", y* "**a**": "*Conocer y apreciar los valores y las normas de convivencia, aprender a obrar de acuerdo con ellas, prepararse para el ejercicio activo de la ciudadanía y respetar los derechos humanos, así como el pluralismo propio de una sociedad democrática*".

Dentro de las **Competencias Clave** destacamos las **Competencias sociales y cívicas**, utilizando las actividades deportivas para fomentar los valores de convivencia, compañerismo, relaciones sociales... o **Competencias básicas en ciencia y tecnología**, fomentando valores de utilización correcta del medio ambiente contribuyendo a su conservación y mejora".

También reflejamos que en ésta actividad, los alumnos van a poner en práctica **contenidos** trabajados dentro de las clases de EF, podemos destacar: Valores del deporte. Juego limpio. Cuidado del entorno natural. Valoración del deporte como herramienta para la resolución de situaciones conflictivas. Así como **el criterio de evaluación nº 9.** Opinar coherentemente con actitud crítica tanto desde la perspectiva de participante como de espectador, ante las posibles situaciones conflictivas surgidas, participando en debates, y aceptando las opiniones de los demás, y el **estándar de aprendizaje evaluable 9.3.** Muestra buena disposición para solucionar los conflictos de manera razonable.

4.2. METODOLOGÍA

En nuestra labor docente y a la hora de poner en práctica nuestra sesión, deberemos procurar que el aprendizaje de nuestros alumnos/as sea significativo, con un carácter lúdico y global, mediante una enseñanza individualizada y atendiendo a la diversidad del alumnado.

En este sentido, podemos destacar algunas de las **Orientaciones metodológicas** que se citan **en la Introducción del Anexo de E.F. del D89/2014,** por ejemplo, favorecer el trabajo libre, usar una práctica y progresiva en la actividad, dosificando el esfuerzo desde actividades más cortas y frecuentes hasta las de mayor duración y aprovechar las posibilidades del lenguaje corporal favoreciendo actividades como la danza y, en general, las de expresión corporal.

Así mismo, también tendremos en cuenta lo establecido en la **Orden 65/2015 en su anexo II** que establece orientaciones metodológicas para el trabajo por competencias en el aula y recomienda utilizar metodologías activas como del aprendizaje cooperativo, el aprendizaje por proyectos o el aprendizaje basado en problemas.

4.3. TEMPORALIZACIÓN Y RECURSOS

Esta jornada de convivencia se llama "***A jugar todos al Parque***". Una vez reunidos los responsables del desarrollo de la actividad con tutores y equipo directivo, se fijan el 17 de junio (para los cursos de 1º, 2º y 3º de Primaria, siguiendo los criterios marcados por jefatura de estudios y para garantizar el adecuado desarrollo de las actividades) y el **18 de junio** (para los cursos de 4º, 5º y 6º de Primaria), es decir al finalizar el **tercer trimestre**, para su realización y se ajustan las distintas responsabilidades y funciones para que la actividad sea un éxito como en el curso anterior:

- ***Policía local***: velar por la seguridad en el desplazamiento al parque.

- ***AMPA y Asociación de amas de casa***: preparar y degustar un almuerzo sano (pan tomata, fruta y un dulce típico de la localidad) para todos los participantes.

- ***Docentes acompañantes***: velar por el orden durante el desplazamiento y colaborar en la realización de las actividades deportivas que se llevarán a cabo durante la jornada.

- ***Maestros de Educación Física***: responsables de la organización y correcto desarrollo de las actividades.

- ***Alumnos responsables***: encargados de llevar y recoger el material necesario que vamos a utilizar.

En este sentido, para la correcta realización de la jornada de convivencia son necesarios varios **recursos:**

Humanos:

- Policía local, alguaciles y protección civil que garanticen la seguridad del desplazamiento y aporten coches de apoyo.
- Docentes: aportan seguridad en el desplazamiento y apoyan a los profesores de EF en la organización y control de las actividades que se van a desarrollar.
- AMPA y Asociación de amas de casa: se encargan de la preparación del desayuno sano y su traslado.
- Alumnos-ayuda: encargados de ayudar y animar a los "alumnos especiales".
- Alumnos responsables del material: encargados de su transporte y control.

Materiales: petancas, pelotas de goma espuma, discos, palas, sogas, pañuelos, mapas y hojas de control. Los alumnos deben de aportar vestimenta y calzado adecuado, gorra... Aquellos alumnos que se desplazan en bici deben llevar casco y chaleco reflectante.

Permisos: autorizaciones familiares, autorización del ayuntamiento. Al estar la actividad recogida en el Programa deportivo del Centro y la PGA no se necesita ya el visto bueno del Consejo escolar.

4.4. INTERDISCIPLINARIEDAD Y ELEMENTOS TRANSVERSALES

Con este supuesto se puede plantear un **trabajo interdisciplinar** con otras áreas, por ejemplo, con **Ciencias Naturales** en el cuidado y respeto del medio ambiente o con **Educación Artística** para la realización de dibujos, pancartas, materiales, etc.

Por otro lado, siguiendo el **RD 126/2014,** a través de estas actividades trabajamos una serie de contenidos que pueden ser trabajados desde todas las áreas, conocidos como **elementos transversales,** principalmente igualdad efectiva entre hombres y mujeres, prevención y resolución pacífica de conflictos, desarrollo sostenible y el medio ambiente, educación y seguridad vial....

4.5. ATENCIÓN A LA DIVERSIDAD

Como ya se ha comentado, entre los participantes se encuentran diversos "alumnos especiales" que requieren adoptar una serie de medidas para que puedan realizar correctamente la actividad, siguiendo lo marcado en el Plan de Atención a la Diversidad y en la programación de EF.

- Un alumno de 4º curso, es un niño que está en silla de ruedas. En este caso realizará el desplazamiento por zona asfaltada al paraje ayudado cuando sea necesario por un "alumno-ayuda" y un docente. Después participará en los juegos populares adoptando las medidas necesarias al igual que se hizo en las sesiones de la unidad didáctica (pillao con ayuda, pelota quemada, petanca...).

- Una alumna de 4º curso, es una chica con retraso mental, y al igual que ya pasó en las sesiones de juegos populares y/o tradicionales de la unidad didáctica que acaban de impartir, no presenta mayores problemas porque ya conoce los juegos, recibe la ayuda de una "alumna-ayuda" y siguiendo indicaciones apropiadas por parte del profesor y ánimos constantes, la diversión está garantizada.

- Un alumno de 5º curso, es un chico con retraso mental. En este caso, lo importante es incluirlo en un equipo donde se encuentre cómodo (amigos y alumno-ayuda) para realizar los juegos alternativos. A nivel físico no presenta problemas pues tiene unos niveles altos de condición física. Los compañeros y maestros siguen las mismas pautas organizativas y comunicativas que en las sesiones de EF.

- Un alumno de 6º curso, es un chico que tiene roto el tobillo, lleva una escayola y bajo prescripción médica debe estar un tiempo sin hacer actividad física. En este caso, el alumno se desplaza al paraje en el coche de protección oficial o alguacil. Nos ayudará en la mesa de control del circuito de orientación, repartiendo hojas de control, planos, tomando tiempos... Posteriormente, jugará a la petanca sentado.

4.6. PROGRAMA DEPORTIVO DE CENTRO

Partiendo del **Decreto 89/2014** por el que se establece que todos los centros de la comunidad de Madrid deben realizar un Proyecto Deportivo, nuestro centro viene desarrollando durante el presente curso un **Proyectos Escolar Saludable,** el cual se compone de gran cantidad de actividades encaminadas a conseguir la formación integral y a la mejora de la calidad de vida y la salud de nuestros alumnos/as.

Entre los objetivos que pretendemos conseguir con nuestro Proyecto "Nuestro colegio se mueve" podemos destacar:

- Aumentar la práctica físico-deportiva diaria del alumnado.
- Educar en valores: participación, solidaridad, respeto...
- Aumentar el bagaje motriz de nuestros alumnos/as.
- Crear hábitos saludables (higienes, postura, alimentación...)

Dentro de este proyecto encontramos diversas actividades deportivas que se desarrollarán a lo largo del curso encaminadas a la mejora de la salud y la consolidación de hábitos higiénicos y posturales. En el siguiente apartado analizaremos algunas de ellas.

4.7. DESARROLLO DE LAS ACTIVIDADES

Como ya se ha comentado anteriormente, incluiremos en la PGA y en el Proyecto Deportivo Saludable aquellas actividades e intenciones que pretendemos desarrollar durante este curso. En este sentido, **todos los docentes** del centro podrán hacer sus aportaciones en las **reuniones de nivel**, las cuales se llevarán a **CCP** y, por último, aprobadas por el **claustro.** Las actuaciones que se van a desarrollar son de tres tipos:

Actuaciones previas: Una vez fijada la fecha de su realización se realizan las siguientes actuaciones:

- Se fija la duración de la jornada, de 11:00 h a 14:00h (***hora de salida*** a las 11:00h y ***hora de regreso*** a las 13:40h) y se ven los profesores implicados para comentarles la actividad y sus funciones.
- Se habla con el ***AMPA y la Asociación de Amas de casa*** para la elaboración del almuerzo sano.
- Se habla con la ***policía local y protección civil*** para garantizar la seguridad en el desplazamiento.
- Se redacta una ***carta a las familias*** explicándoles la jornada y los materiales que sus hijos e hijas deben de aportar: en caso de desplazarse en bici es obligatorio el casco y el chaleco reflectante, calzado adecuado, mochila, ropa de abrigo, gorra, agua, crema... Además, se publica todo lo relacionado con la jornada en el Blog de EF del centro.
- Se nombran los ***alumnos responsables del material***. También se nombran a los alumnos y maestros que van a ayudar a los "alumnos especiales".
- Los ***maestros de Educación Física*** fijan las actividades a desarrollar: los ***alumnos de 4º curso*** realizarán juegos populares y/o

tradicionales (sogatira, carrera de sacos, pañuelo, petanca, la cadena, pillaos, pelota quemada...) que han aprendido y practicado en la unidad didáctica que han trabajado anteriormente. Los ***alumnos de 5º curso*** realizarán juegos alternativos (ultimate, palas...) que han trabajado en la unidad didáctica del 3er trimestre. Los ***alumnos de 6º curso*** realizarán una carrera de orientación en grupos de 3 en un circuito marcado con anterioridad, aprovechando los conocimientos adquiridos en la unidad didáctica que acaban de realizar. Posteriormente se unirán a sus compañeros y se divertirán con los juegos populares y alternativos.

- Los maestros de Educación Física organizarán los diferentes equipos mezclando los alumn@ de las dos líneas para fomentar la convivencia: en 4º y 5º equipos para realizar el circuito de juegos populares y juegos alternativos, y en 6º curso equipos de 3 alumn@s para realizar el circuito de orientación. En los agrupamientos se tendrán en cuenta a los "alumnos especiales" para garantizar su participación e integración.

Actuaciones durante la jornada de convivencia

- El día 18 de junio, los alumn@s y docentes comienzan su jornada escolar a las **9:00h** de forma normalizada. Los alumn@s que se van a desplazar en bici dejan la bici, casco y chaleco en la zona habilitada.
- A las **11:00h** acaba la 2ª clase y los alumn@s dejan el material escolar en sus clases, cogen su mochila y salen a la puerta del centro. Los alumn@s que van en bici hacen lo propio también. En la puerta del centro están ya los docentes participantes, alguaciles y policía local. Los alumn@s responsables del material se hacen cargo de él (en este caso lo portan ellos, si hubiera algún material pesado se trasladaría en el coche de la policía local o alguaciles).
- A las **11:10h** se inicia el desplazamiento al Chortal, encabezada la marcha por el coche de la policía local y cerrada por un alguacil en moto. Los alumnos que se desplazan en bici acompañados por 3-4 docentes inician también el recorrido ya que éstos harán una vuelta por el paraje para hacer tiempo a que lleguen los demás. El tiempo total del desplazamiento será de 20 min. aprox, respetando siempre las normas de circulación (educación vial).
- A las **11:30h** aprox se llega al Chortal, se dejan las cosas en la zona habilitada y las madres del AMPA y Asociación de amas de casa reparten el almuerzo saludable (el traslado del almuerzo se organiza convenientemente).

- A las **12:00h** aprox los alumn@s de 4º y 5º se desplazan a la zona de juegos populares y alternativos y los alumn@s de 6º se desplazan a la salida del circuito de orientación. Los docentes encargados y profesores de EF ya han preparado todo lo necesario para el comienzo de las actividades.
- De **12:00h a 13:40h** los alumn@s disfrutan realizando las actividades programadas de forma relajada y divertida, recordando en todo momento que el objetivo principal es la convivencia, diversión, compañerismo...
- A las **13:40h** aprox se inicia el regreso al centro (antes se ha realizado una "batida" para comprobar que todo se queda en perfectas condiciones). Los alumn@s en bici vuelven a hacer un recorrido por el paraje para coincidir con el resto en la llegada al centro.
- A las **14:00h** aprox llegada al centro, recogida de sus materiales escolares y fin de la actividad. Los alumnos responsables dejan el material en su lugar correspondiente.

Actuaciones al finalizar la jornada de convivencia:

Los responsables de la actividad redactan un informe evaluativo reflejando lo positivo de la jornada y aquellos aspectos que deben mejorarse de cara a futuras actividades. Se informa a jefatura de estudios y a la CCP del desarrollo de la actividad. El informe evaluativo es recogido en la Memoria final del programa deportivo. También se harán los agradecimientos correspondientes a los agentes colaboradores.

CASO PRÁCTICO Nº4

Plantea una unidad didáctica de 8 sesiones donde se trabaje un deporte colectivo. Las sesiones irán dirigidas a un grupo de 5º de primaria con 25 alumnos donde encontramos dos alumnos inmigrantes y un alumno hiperactivo.

1. INTRODUCCIÓN

El contenido de este problema es muy importante dentro de la E.F., pues trata aspectos fundamentales en nuestra área como **la iniciación a los deportes colectivos,** aspectos que se desarrollan más ampliamente en el **tema 14,** donde se analiza el deporte como actividad educativa y la didáctica, así como sus aspectos técnicos y tácticos.

A través de la enseñanza adecuada de los deportes colectivos con carácter educativo, desarrollaremos la competencia motriz de nuestros alumnos, les dotaremos de valores de superación, responsabilidad, trabajo en equipo, deportividad y respeto a los compañeros y adversarios, e insistiremos en calentamientos adecuados, pautas alimenticias, higiene postural, prevención de accidentes...

Por otro lado, para comprender mejor el contenido de este supuesto analizaremos una serie de conceptos que son inherentes al enunciado del mismo:

Unidad Didáctica: Jesús Viciana la define como "la unidad mínima del currículum del alumno con pleno sentido en sí misma, aunque contiene unidades más pequeñas que son las sesiones".

Sesión: Según **Pieron**, "es el punto de unión entre la programación, a veces muy teórica, y la realidad de la clase".

Deporte colectivo: Según **Parlebás** son *"aquellos en los que se participa o compite en equipo, entendiendo como equipo la unión de varios jugadores para conseguir un mismo objetivo, realizando una serie de acciones reglamentadas en colaboración, cooperación y participación de todos, tratando de vencer la oposición de los contrarios o adversarios que igualmente se organizan en equipo con el mismo fin".*

ACNEAE (Decreto 89/2014, artículo 17): "Se considera ACNEAE todo aquellos alumnos que requieran una atención educativa diferente a la ordinaria por presentar necesidades educativas especiales por discapacidad, por dificultades específicas de aprendizaje (entre ellas la dislexia), por presentar Trastorno por Déficit de Atención e Hiperactividad

(TDAH), por sus altas capacidades intelectuales, por su incorporación tardía al sistema educativo, o por condiciones personales o de historia escolar." (Sólo si el supuesto presenta un ACNEAE).

Hecha esta breve introducción pasaremos a analizar el segundo apartado de este supuesto.

2. MARCO LEGISLATIVO

La sesión que se nos pide, así como la U.D. en la que se enmarca, queda perfectamente justificada mediante la legislación vigente para el curso 2016/17 en nuestra comunidad de CLM a través de: **Ley Orgánica 8/2013 (LOMCE)**, **Ley Orgánica de Educación (LOE)**, el **Real Decreto 126/2014,** por el que se establece el **currículo básico de la Educación Primaria a nivel nacional**, y más concretamente el **Decreto 89/2014,** por el que se establece **el currículo de la Educación Primaria en la Comunidad de Madrid.**

Además, tendremos en cuenta otra como:

- **Orden ECD65/2015** (relación de contenidos, criterios de evaluación y competencias)

- **ORDEN 1493/2015,** por la que se regula la evaluación y la promoción de los alumnos con necesidad específica de apoyo educativo

- **Orden 3622/2014,** por la que se regulan determinados aspectos de organización y funcionamiento, así como la evaluación y los documentos de aplicación en la Educación Primaria

- ***Decreto 15/2007,*** *por el que se establece el marco regulador de la convivencia en los centros docentes de la Comunidad de Madrid.*

- **LEY 2/2010,** de **Autoridad del Profesor**.

Teniendo en cuenta este marco legislativo, pasaremos a contextualizar este supuesto práctico.

3. CONTEXTUALIZACIÓN

El centro en el que se desarrollará la sesión está situado en la **Comunidad de Madrid** y cuenta con 499 alumnos, además **el centro cuenta con jornada continuada de 9 a 14 horas** Esta sesión se impartirá en el grupo **5ºA**, formado por **25 alumnos, 14 chicos y 11 chicas.** En general, el grupo es bastante participativo en las actividades de E.F.

Estos alumnos se encuentran en un intervalo de edad que oscila entre los 10 y 11 años. Algunas de sus **características psicoevolutivas** más destacadas son:

A nivel cognitivo: Se sitúan en el estadio de las operaciones formales de Piaget, lo que les permite realizar operaciones mentales abstractas.

A nivel socio-afectivo: Empiezan progresivamente a independizarse de los adultos, aumentando su autonomía y afianzando su personalidad.

A nivel motriz: Comienzan los procesos característicos de la pubertad (crecimiento, aumento de musculatura, etc.). Consolidad su esquema corporal y toman conciencia global de su cuerpo, sistematizan hábitos higiénicos y respetan las medidas de seguridad.

Dentro del grupo encontramos **tres alumnos que presentan unas características especiales** que deberemos tener en cuenta.

Una vez analizado el contexto, pasaremos a analizar la intervención educativa del supuesto que se nos pide.

4. INTERVENCIÓN EDUCATIVA

4.1. RELACIÓN CON EL CURRÍCULUM

Con el trabajo de esta Unidad Didáctica contribuiremos a conseguir **diversos elementos curriculares** marcados en el **D.89/2014**, tales como el/los **Objetivo/s de Etapa "k":** Valorar la higiene y la salud, conocer y respetar el cuerpo humano, y utilizar la educación física y el deporte como medios para favorecer el desarrollo personal y social".

*A*sí como **las Competencias Clave Sociales y cívicas** a través de aprender a trabajar en equipo, a expresar y comprender puntos de vista diferentes, empatía, tolerancia..., y la de **aprender a aprender**, fomentando el esfuerzo por aprender individual y colectivamente, ser capaz de superar los obstáculos y las situaciones problemas que se les plantean...

También podemos destacar el **contenido: "Iniciación a las tácticas de defensa y ataque en los juegos".** Así como el **Criterio de Evaluación nº3**: *""Resolver retos tácticos elementales propios del juego y de actividades físicas, con o sin oposición, aplicando principios y reglas para resolver las situaciones motrices, actuando de forma individual, coordinada y cooperativa y desempeñando las diferentes funciones implícitas en juegos y actividades"*, y los **estándares de aprendizaje evaluables: 3.1.** *"Utiliza los recursos adecuados para resolver situaciones básicas de táctica individual y colectiva en diferentes situaciones motrices"* y **3.2.** *"Realiza combinaciones* *de habilidades motrices básicas ajustándose a un objetivo y a unos parámetros espacio-temporales"*, entre otros.

4.2. METODOLOGÍA

En nuestra labor docente y a la hora de poner en práctica nuestra sesión, deberemos procurar que el aprendizaje de nuestros alumnos/as sea significativo, con un carácter lúdico y global, mediante una enseñanza individualizada y atendiendo a la diversidad del alumnado.

En este sentido, podemos destacar algunas de las **Orientaciones metodológicas** que se citan **en la Introducción del Anexo de E.F. del D89/2014,** por ejemplo, favorecer el trabajo libre, usar una práctica y progresiva en la actividad, dosificando el esfuerzo desde actividades más cortas y frecuentes hasta las de mayor duración y aprovechar las posibilidades del lenguaje corporal favoreciendo actividades como la danza y, en general, las de expresión corporal.

Así mismo, también tendremos en cuenta lo establecido en la **Orden 65/2015 en su anexo II** que establece orientaciones metodológicas para el trabajo por competencias en el aula y recomienda utilizar metodologías activas como del aprendizaje cooperativo, el aprendizaje por proyectos o el aprendizaje basado en problemas.

En cuanto a los **estilos de enseñanza** que utilizaremos serán fundamentalmente la resolución de problemas, el descubrimiento guiado y la asignación de tareas. Trabajaremos diversos tipos de **agrupamientos** y las **instalaciones y materiales** serán los propios del área y los que puedan aportar los alumnos/as.

4.3. TEMPORALIZACIÓN Y RECURSOS

La **Unidad Didáctica** lleva el nombre de **"Nos gusta el baloncesto"** y es una de las 12 unidades que se encuentran enmarcadas dentro de nuestra programación didáctica, en concreto es la **UD número 7**, la cual consta de **8 sesiones** y se desarrolla en el **tercer trimestre.**

La secuenciación de estas sesiones es la siguiente:

- **Sesión 1:** "¿A qué jugamos hoy?"
- **Sesión 2:** "¿Qué es el baloncesto?"
- **Sesión 3:** "A divertirse con el basket"
- **Sesión 4:** "Bota, bota, bota"

- **Sesión 5:** "¿Me la pasas?"
- **Sesión 6: "**Practico el tiro"
- **Sesión 7:** "Es mejor jugar y pasarlo bien"
- **Sesión 8:** "Mini-competiciones"

A continuación, desarrollaremos la **sesión nº 8.**

En cuanto a los **recursos** de nuestro centro para la realización de esta U.D., contamos con un pabellón cubierto y dos pistas polideportivas al aire libre, las cuales cumplen con la normativa establecida en el **RD 132/2010.**

En cuanto al **material,** nuestra área cuenta con el material suficiente y necesario para impartir correctamente las sesiones de esta U.D., por ejemplo: balones de baloncesto de diferente tamaño, canastas de diversas alturas (dos canastas oficiales, cuatro de minibasket y cuatro de balonkorf), etc. Así como el material propio de los alumnos: zapatillas, ropa deportiva, bosa de aseo; y del maestro para la gestión, organización y control de la clase.

También destacamos el **uso de las TIC**, por ejemplo: El proyector y la pantalla digital para el visionado de videos y explicaciones, los Netbook de los alumnos/as para la realización de un trabajo de investigación y la práctica de juegos interactivos, etc.

4.4. INTERDISCIPLINARIEDAD Y ELEMENTOS TRANSVERSALES

A través de esta Unidad se puede plantear un **trabajo interdisciplinar** con otras áreas, por ejemplo con la de **Inglés**, donde se puede comprender el significado de muchas palabras de jerga baloncestística como dribling, basket, etc...; con el área de **Matemáticas** con el uso de los números para llevar la puntuación en los juegos y para entender algunas reglas..., o **Ciencias Naturales** en el conocimiento del cuerpo humano y pautas saludables.

Además, esta Unidad Didáctica se encuentra estrechamente relacionada con el **PROYECTO DEPORTIVO** que desarrolla nuestro centro *"El colegio se mueve",* donde los alumnos tienen la posibilidad de practicar baloncesto en los recreos, fiestas de finales de trimestre, partidillo contra los maestros y maestras, etc. Además, los alumnos van a asistir a una actividad donde jugadores de baloncesto en silla de ruedas dan una charla y se practican diversos juegos.

Por otro lado, siguiendo el **RD 126/2014 (o el D.89/2014 en su artículo 8),** a través de esta U.D. trabajamos una serie de contenidos que pueden ser trabajados desde todas las áreas, conocidos como **elementos transversales,** principalmente la educación en valores y la práctica diaria del ejercicio físico para favorecer una vida activa, saludable y autónoma.

4.5. EVALUACIÓN

Según la **Orden 3622/2014,** y lo establecido en nuestra programación, la **evaluación de nuestro alumnado será continua y global**, siendo evaluados en todas las sesiones a través de diferentes estándares de aprendizaje evaluables. Dichos estándares son los siguientes:

3.1. Utiliza los recursos adecuados para resolver situaciones básicas de táctica individual y colectiva en diferentes situaciones motrices.

3.2. Realiza combinaciones de habilidades motrices básicas ajustándose a un objetivo y a unos parámetros espacio-temporales.

9.3. Muestra buena disposición para solucionar los conflictos de manera razonable.

9.4. Reconoce y califica negativamente las conductas inapropiadas que se producen en la práctica o en los espectáculos deportivos.

12.1. Utiliza las nuevas tecnologías para localizar y extraer la información que se le solicita.

12.2. Presenta sus trabajos atendiendo a las pautas proporcionadas, con orden, estructura y limpieza y utilizando programas de presentación.

13.1. Tiene interés por mejorar la competencia motriz.

13.2. Demuestra autonomía y confianza en diferentes situaciones, resolviendo problemas motores con espontaneidad y creatividad.

13.3. Incorpora en sus rutinas el cuidado e higiene del cuerpo.

13.4. Participa en la recogida y organización de material utilizado en las clases.

13.5. Acepta formar parte del grupo que le corresponda y el resultado de las competiciones con deportividad.

Para valorar la consecución de estos estándares se utilizarán diferentes **instrumentos de evaluación** como el registro anecdotario, las listas de control, rúbrica o el portfolio.

Cabe destacar que la evaluación se llevará a cabo tanto con los alumnos, como con el proceso de enseñanza y la propia práctica docente.

4.6. ATENCIÓN A LA DIVERSIDAD

Para atender correctamente a todo el alumnado seguiremos lo marcado en la normativa que regula la atención personalizada del alumnado en nuestra comunidad a través del ***Orden 1493/2015,*** destacando la **coordinación** necesaria con el equipo de orientación, jefatura de estudios, tutor, familias...

Como dijimos en la contextualización del grupo, encontramos **dos alumnos inmigrantes**, que llevan 4 años y 7 meses en el centro, respectivamente. Uno de ellos es de origen argentino y está perfectamente integrado en el centro y en la vida española. El otro es de origen rumano y todavía está en proceso de adaptación, aunque a nivel comunicativo se resuelve a través de su dominio básico del castellano y de la lengua inglesa, la cual domina bastante bien. Este alumno recibe apoyo por parte de los especialistas para el aprendizaje del castellano y lleva un **ACI** donde se reflejan esas medidas de acceso al currículo y a la comunicación. En EF adoptamos varias medidas como, por ejemplo: traducción de fichas a su idioma, ejemplos prácticos de algunos ejercicios, incluirlo en un grupo adecuado..., ya que el alumno a nivel físico y motriz no presenta ninguna dificultad, además de gustarle mucho el deporte.

Por otro lado, también tenemos un alumno **diagnosticado hiperactivo (TDAH).** Una vez conocido su informe médico, a través de la coordinación con el orientador, el tutor, jefatura de estudios y reunidos con la familia, decir que realiza la EF con normalidad, ya que está perfectamente medicado. A lo largo de las sesiones estamos pendientes de proporcionarle motivación constante, darle diversos roles, fomentar su concentración y trabajo, no presentando ningún problema para seguir el desarrollo de las sesiones.

4.7. DESARROLLO DE LA SESIÓN

Hecho este análisis de la U.D., pasaremos a desarrollar la sesión mencionada anteriormente. En esta sesión realizaremos mini-partidillos de baloncesto por equipos y recogeremos los trabajos que solicitamos a los alumnos en la primera sesión. Además, mientras los alumnos/as juegan realizaremos una prueba práctica para comprobar su evolución, la cual valoraremos con una rúbrica.

En primer lugar, analizaremos algunos aspectos a tener en cuenta:

- **Duración**: 1 hora
- **Instalación**: Pista polideportiva

- **Material:** Balones, canastas, petos...
- **Contenidos:** "Utilización de juegos deportivos modificados y mini-deportes", "Estrategias de cooperación, oposición y cooperación/oposición", "Realización de juegos y de actividades deportivas", "Aceptación y respeto hacia las normas, reglas, estrategias y personas que participan en el juego", "Valoración del esfuerzo personal y colectivo".
- **Objetivos didácticos:**
  - Adaptar las habilidades de manipulación de objetos a diferentes actividades
  - Incorporar en sus rutinas el cuidado e higiene del cuerpo.
  - Participar en la recogida y organización de material utilizado.
  - Aceptar formar parte del grupo que le corresponda y el resultado de las competiciones con deportividad.
  - Utilizar las nuevas tecnologías para localizar y extraer la información.
  - Presentar sus trabajos atendiendo a unas pautas establecidas

- **Metodología: Asignación de tareas, resolución de problemas**
- **Competencias Clave**: Sociales y cívicas, Aprender a aprender
- **Evaluación: Estándares de aprendizaje e instrumentos de evaluación**
  - **3.1, 3.2 – Rúbrica**
  - **13.1, 13.2, 13.3, 13.4, 13.5 – Registro anecdotario**
  - **12.1, 12.2 – Portfolio (trabajo teórico)**

Hecho este análisis de la sesión, a continuación, pasaremos a su desarrollo, el cual dividiremos en 3 partes:

1ª PARTE: ANIMACIÓN Y CALENTAMIENTO (10'-15')

La sesión comenzará en el aula de los alumnos, donde pasaremos lista, revisaremos que traen el material adecuado (chándal y bolsa de aseo), se nombran los encargados y recogemos los trabajos teóricos individuales sobre la U.D. Después, explicaremos que en la sesión de hoy se realizará una evaluación sobre sus habilidades motrices relacionadas con el baloncesto y una serie de partidillos de 3x3 (un equipo será de 4).

Posteriormente, seguiremos las rutinas diarias de ir en orden y silencio hasta la pista polideportiva, donde ya encontramos el material necesario.

Hacemos el primer juego de la sesión que nos servirá para hacer los grupos o equipos para la parte principal: "Haz lo que yo digo". La última indicación será hacer grupos de 3 (y uno de 4). Cuando tengamos los grupos le repartiremos petos de diferente color a cada uno.

2ª PARTE: PARTE PRINCIPAL (35'-40')

En esta parte realizaremos 2 actividades. Por un lado, el maestro pasará la prueba práctica de 2 en 2 alumnos/as. Y, por otro, los demás alumnos/as realizarán partidillos de 3x3 a una canasta (normas ya explicadas anteriormente).

En otra canasta el maestro pasará y evaluará la **prueba práctica:**

- Zig-zag entre conos (botando)

- Pases y recepciones

- Tiro a canasta

- Entrada a canasta

Los niveles de logro de la **rúbrica** irán del 1 al 5, siendo 1 como "no aceptable" y el 5 "excelente":

ESTÁNDAR/ ALUMNO	NO CONSEGUIDO	ACEPTA-BLE	BUENO	MUY BUENO	EXCELENTE
2.1.3	1	2	3	4	5
ALUMNO 1					
ALUMNO 2					

A los alumnos/as se les irá llamando de 2 en 2, siendo estos siempre de equipos distintos con el fin de no desnivelar los equipos.

3ª PARTE: PARTE FINAL Y VUELTA A LA CALMA (5'-10')

Terminamos la sesión con la recogida del material, el feed-back sobre la sesión y las labores higiénicas. Por último, volvemos al aula en fila y en silencio.

NOTAS ACLARATORIAS A LA SESIÓN.

En todo momento prestaremos especial atención al alumno con TDAH para que participe con normalidad en los partidos. En cuanto al alumno rumano, el primer juego lo haremos con gestos y diremos los números en español y en inglés. Para la prueba práctica le haremos una demostración previa.

CASO PRÁCTICO Nº5

Describe el trabajo planteado a lo largo de un curso para un grupo de 25 alumnos/as, así como diferentes tareas o actividades plasmadas en una sesión que estén relacionadas con la consolidación de hábitos de higiene corporal y postural que beneficien la calidad de vida y la salud del alumnado.

1. INTRODUCCIÓN

El contenido de esta situación es muy importante dentro de la E.F., pues trata sobre una de las prioridades que todos los centros educativos deberían incluir en su P.G.A. como es la salud y la calidad de vida de nuestro alumnado. Concretamente, estos contenidos tienen un tratamiento mucho más amplio en el tema 5 de nuestro temario de oposición de E.F.

El propósito de la actividad física, así como de la E.F. y sus correspondientes especialistas, consiste en mejorar el estado de la condición física y la salud de nuestro alumnado. Para ello, a lo largo de todo el curso realizaremos una serie de tareas o actividades con el objetivo de transmitir y crear en ellos y ellas unos hábitos de vida sana y saludable. Estas actividades estarán incluidas en nuestro Proyecto Deportivo de centro "Nuestro colegio se mueve".

Por otro lado, para comprender mejor el contenido de este supuesto analizaremos una serie de conceptos que se encuentran estrechamente relacionados con el enunciado del mismo.

En primer lugar, la **PGA** es un documento propio y específico de cada centro educativo donde se recogen los objetivos que se persiguen en el curso actual, así como las medidas o acciones para conseguirlos.

Por otro lado, según **Pieron** una **sesión** "es el punto de unión entre la programación, a veces muy teórica, y la realidad de la clase". Las sesiones las incluimos en **Unidades Didácticas,** que según **Jesús Viciana** son "la unidad mínima del currículum del alumno con pleno sentido en sí misma, aunque contiene unidades más pequeñas que son las sesiones".

También debemos destacar el concepto de **Programa o Proyecto Deportivo Escolar,** el cual se define como el conjunto de actividades físicas y deportivas que se realizan en el centro educativo, en horario lectivo y no lectivo, con el fin de promover e inculcar un estilo de vida saludable a través del deporte.

Por último, el concepto alrededor del cual gira todo el supuesto es el de **salud,** que la **OMS y Terris** definen como "e estado de completo bienestar físico, mental y social, y no solamente la ausencia de afecciones o invalideces".

Hecha esta breve introducción pasaremos a analizar el segundo apartado de este supuesto.

2. MARCO LEGISLATIVO

La contenido de este supuesto queda perfectamente justificado mediante la legislación vigente para el curso 2016/17 en nuestra comunidad de Castilla-La Mancha a través de: **Ley Orgánica 8/2013** (**LOMCE**), **Ley Orgánica de Educación** (**LOE**), la **Ley 7/2010, de Educación de Castilla-La Mancha**, el **Real Decreto 126/2014,** por el que se establece el **currículo básico de la Educación Primaria a nivel nacional**, y más concretamente el **Decreto 54/2014,** por el que se establece **el currículo de la Educación Primaria en CLM.**

Además, tendremos en cuenta otra normativa como:

- **D.66/2013** de atención a la diversidad en CLM

- **Orden 5/08/2014** de organización y evaluación de Primaria en CLM

- **Resolución 11/03/15** (categorización y ponderación de estándares)

- **Orden ECD65/2015** (relación de contenidos, criterios de evaluación y competencias)

Teniendo en cuenta este marco legislativo, pasaremos a contextualizar este supuesto práctico.

3. CONTEXTUALIZACIÓN

El centro en el que se desarrollará estas actividades está situado en la Comunidad de Castilla-La Mancha y cuenta con 499 alumnos. El curso elegido para su desarrollo es **5º de Primaria**, formado por **25 alumnos, 14 chicos y 11 chicas.** En general, el grupo es bastante participativo en las actividades de E.F.

Estos alumnos se encuentran en un intervalo de edad que oscila entre los 10 y 11 años. Algunas de sus **características psicoevolutivas** más destacadas son:

A nivel cognitivo: Se sitúan en el estadio de las operaciones formales de Piaget, lo que les permite realizar operaciones mentales abstractas.

A nivel socio-afectivo: Empiezan progresivamente a independizarse de los adultos, aumentando su autonomía y afianzando su personalidad.

A nivel motriz: Comienzan los procesos característicos de la pubertad (crecimiento, aumento de musculatura, etc.). Consolidad su esquema corporal y toman conciencia global de su cuerpo, sistematizan hábitos higiénicos y respetan las medidas de seguridad.

Una vez analizado el contexto, pasaremos a analizar la intervención educativa del supuesto que se nos pide.

4. INTERVENCIÓN EDUCATIVA

4.1. RELACIÓN CON EL CURRÍCULUM

En primer lugar, podemos destacar que la **LOMCE en su Disposición adicional cuarta** señala que: "Las administraciones educativas adoptarán medidas para que la **actividad física** y la **dieta equilibrada** formen parte del comportamiento infantil y juvenil. A estos efectos, promoverán la práctica diaria de **deporte y ejercicio** durante la jornada escolar...". De aquí se desprende la justificación o necesidad de elaboración de los proyectos deportivos en los centros escolares.

Por otro lado, con el trabajo del contenido de este supuesto se contribuye a la consecución de **diversos elementos curriculares** marcados en el **D.54/2014**, tales como el **Objetivo General de Etapa "k"**: "*"Valorar la higiene y la salud, aceptar el propio cuerpo y el de los otros, respetar las diferencias y utilizar la educación física y el deporte como medios para favorecer el desarrollo personal y social", o* **las Competencias Clave Sociales y cívicas y** a través las interacciones sociales que se dan en los juegos y actividades, o **sentido de iniciativa y espíritu emprendedor**, fomentando la adquisición de autonomía del alumnado en el cuidado del cuerpo e higiene personal, entre otras.

También podemos destacar el **Bloque de Contenidos nº1 "Actividad física y salud"** que se trabaja en todos los cursos de Primaria, con contenidos como: "Cuidado del cuerpo", "adquisición de hábitos higiénicos", "respeto de las diferentes realidades corporales", "hábitos de alimentación", etc.

Así mismo, podemos destacar el **Criterio de Evaluación nº2** que se trabaja en 5º de Primaria: "Identificar algunos de los efectos del ejercicio físico, la higiene, la alimentación y los hábitos posturales sobre la salud", y su **estándar de aprendizaje evaluable 1.2.3.** "Conoce algunos de los efectos positivos del ejercicio físico para la salud", entre otros.

4.2. METODOLOGÍA

En nuestra labor docente y a la hora de poner en práctica nuestras actividades deberemos tener en cuenta las **orientaciones metodológicas** marcadas en el **D.54/2014** y procurar que el aprendizaje de nuestros alumnos/as sea significativo, con un carácter lúdico y global, mediante una enseñanza individualizada y atendiendo a la diversidad del alumnado.

Así mismo, también tendremos en cuenta lo establecido en la **Orden 65/2015 en su anexo II** que establece orientaciones para el trabajo por competencias en el aula y recomienda utilizar metodologías activas como del aprendizaje cooperativo, el aprendizaje por proyectos o el aprendizaje basado en problemas.

4.3. TEMPORALIZACIÓN Y RECURSOS

Las actividades y tareas relacionadas con la salud que nos pide este supuesto se encuentran incluidas en la **P.G.A.** y en el **Proyecto Deportivo** de nuestro centro, titulado "Nuestro colegio se mueve". Así mismo, se encuentran muy relacionadas con la **U.D. nº12 de nuestra programación "Cuido mi cuerpo",** que se desarrolla de manera transversal a lo largo de todo el curso.

Por otro lado, para la correcta realización de cada actividad serán necesarios varios tipos de recursos:

- Humanos: Docentes, especialistas (fisioterapeuta...), voluntarios, los propios alumnos/as, las familias...
- Materiales: Los propios de E.F. (colchonetas...), los aportados por los voluntarios y especialistas (fruta...), los propios materiales de los alumnos/as (ropa deportiva, bolsa de aseo...), etc.
- Instalaciones: Las propias del centro (aulas, pabellón, sala polivalente...), etc. Las cuales cumplen con la normativa establecida en el **RD 132/2010** de requisitos mínimos.
- Autorizaciones: Documento firmado por los padres donde se recojan las posibles alergias de los niños/as a ciertos alimentos.

- TIC: El proyector y la pantalla digital para el visionado de videos y explicaciones, los Netbook de los alumnos/as para la realización de trabajos de investigación y práctica de juegos interactivos, etc.

4.4. INTERDISCIPLINARIEDAD Y ELEMENTOS TRANSVERSALES

Con este supuesto se puede plantear un **trabajo interdisciplinar** con otras áreas, por ejemplo, con **Ciencias Naturales** en el conocimiento del cuerpo humano y pautas saludables o con **Educación Artística** para la realización de dibujos, pancartas, decoración del aula, etc.

Además, como ya se ha comentado, destacamos la inclusión de estas actividades en el **Proyecto Deportivo** que desarrolla nuestro centro *"El colegio se mueve"*, con actividades que analizaremos en un apartado posteriormente.

Por otro lado, siguiendo el **RD 126/2014,** a través de estas actividades trabajamos una serie de contenidos que pueden ser trabajados desde todas las áreas, conocidos como **elementos transversales,** principalmente con la actividad física y la dieta equilibrada.

4.5. ATENCIÓN A LA DIVERSIDAD

En este apartado debemos tener en cuenta lo establecido en el **Decreto 66/2013** que regula la respuesta a la diversidad del alumnado en CLM, en las medidas de atención a la diversidad establecidas en la PGA y en la programación de E.F.

En este supuesto no encontramos ningún alumno/a con características especiales a destacar, si bien debemos estar preparados por si en algún momento algún alumno/a necesitase de una atención más especializada. Para ello será necesario un contacto y un trabajo coordinado y continuo con los especialistas correspondientes, tutores y familias.

4.6. PROGRAMA DEPORTIVO DE CENTRO

Partiendo de la **Orden de 03/10/2016** por la que se crea y organiza la **Red de Centros Docentes Saludables de CLM,** nuestro centro viene desarrollando durante el presente curso un **Proyectos Escolar Saludable,** el cual se compone de gran cantidad de actividades encaminadas a conseguir la formación integral y a la mejora de la calidad de vida y la salud de nuestros alumnos/as.

Entre los objetivos que pretendemos conseguir con nuestro Proyecto "Nuestro colegio se mueve" podemos destacar:

- Aumentar la práctica físico-deportiva diaria del alumnado.

- Educar en valores: participación, solidaridad, respeto...

- Aumentar el bagaje motriz de nuestros alumnos/as.

- Crear hábitos saludables (higienes, postura, alimentación...)

Dentro de este proyecto encontramos diversas actividades deportivas que se desarrollarán a lo largo del curso encaminadas a la mejora de la salud y la consolidación de hábitos higiénicos y posturales. En el siguiente apartado analizaremos algunas de ellas.

4.7. DESARROLLO DE LAS ACTIVIDADES

Como ya se ha comentado anteriormente, incluiremos en la PGA y en el Proyecto Deportivo Saludable aquellas actividades e intenciones que pretendemos desarrollar durante este curso. En este sentido, **todos los docentes** del centro podrán hacer sus aportaciones en las **reuniones de nivel**, las cuales se llevarán a **CCP** y, por último, aprobadas por el **claustro.**

Algunas de estas actividades son:

- **Los desayunos saludables:** Tanto en Infantil como en Primaria se establecen los alimentos que deben llevar cada día los alumnos/as para la hora del almuerzo: Fruta, lácteos... Se les deja un día de libre elección. Además, en el día de la fruta la fruta es aportada gracias al plan **"La fruta en el colegio".**

- **Control postural:** Al inicio de curso se establece una charla con un fisioterapeuta donde a través de actividades lúdicas y participativas se intentan crear buenos hábitos posturales.

- **Decoración del aula:** Se llevarán a cabo talleres donde se realizarán murales, posters, dibujos, etc., relacionados con los hábitos posturales y la higiene corporal que serán colocados en los pasillos del centro y en el aula.

- **Comunicados a las familias:** A lo largo del curso se entregarán a las familias diversos comunicados con consejos y hábitos de higiene corporal y postural.

- **Otras medidas desde el área de E.F.:** A lo largo de todo el curso desde nuestras sesiones trataremos de prevenir y detectar los posibles problemas corporales de nuestros alumnos/as, así como corregirlos con un programa adaptado elaborado por el especialista correspondiente. También trataremos de inculcar y reforzar los hábitos higiénicos tras la clase de E.F. a través del aseo personal (bolsa de aseo).

Otros aspectos a tener en cuenta: Uso de las TIC, actividades de formación permanente del profesorado (CRFP)...

Es importante que al finalizar cada una de las actividades realizándose elabore un **informe evaluativo** reflejando los aspectos positivos de la misma, así como las que deben mejorarse de cara a futuras actividades similares. También se informará al claustro del desarrollo de las actividades y se darán los agradecimientos oportunos a los colaboradores y responsables. Estos informes los recogeremos en una memoria final del proyecto deportivo.

4.8. DESARROLLO DE UNA SESIÓN

Como dijimos anteriormente, la salud corporal la trabajaremos desde el área de E.F. de manera transversal a lo largo de todo el curso con una U.D. específica de salud. Sin embargo, a continuación, desarrollaremos una sesión perteneciente a la U.D. de Expresión Corporal de nuestra programación, titulada “Estoy hecho un artista”, donde a través de técnicas de expresión y comunicación se desarrollen y trabajen hábitos sanos y saludables.

Esta sesión será la última de la U.D. y en ella se realizarán diferentes representaciones de 4-5 minutos inventadas por los alumnos/as a partir de unas consignas iniciales sobre hábitos posturales, higiénicos, primeros auxilios, etc. Dichas consignas, así como la formación de grupos, se realizaron en la primera sesión de esta U.D.

Se formarán 5 grupos de 5 alumnos/as cada uno y las representaciones girarán en torno a la siguiente temática:

- Grupo 1: Hábitos alimenticios positivos y negativos
- Grupo 2: Primeros auxilios, evacuación y cura de uno o varios heridos.
- Grupo 3: Hábitos posturales (sentarse bien, forma de llevar la mochila...)
- Grupo 4: Aseo personal tras la realización de actividad física, antes de comer...
- Grupo 5: El calentamiento como prevención de lesiones y accidentes.

A continuación, analizaremos algunos aspectos a tener en cuenta de esta sesión:

- **Unidad didáctica: "Estoy hecho un artista"**

- **Nº sesión: 6**

- **Curso: 5ºA**

- **Duración**: 1 hora

- **Instalación**: Sala polivalente multiusos

- **Material:** Los propios de E.F., los aportados por los alumnos/as, fichas evaluativas...

- **Contenidos:** *"La salud corporal", "hábitos higiénicos saludables", "El cuerpo como medio de expresión", "representación de situaciones, ideas, sentimientos y personajes".*

- **Objetivos didácticos:**

- Representar personajes, situaciones, ideas y sentimientos.

- Trabajar en equipo para elaborar una pequeña representación grupal.

- Exponer sus ideas de forma coherente y se expresa de forma correcta.

- Demostrar autonomía y confianza en diferentes situaciones.

- Participar en la recogida y organización de material.

- Aceptar formar parte del grupo que le corresponda.

- **Metodología:** Resolución de problemas

- **Competencias Clave**: Sentido de iniciativa y espíritu emprendedor, Conciencia y expresiones culturales.

- **Evaluación: Estándares de aprendizaje e instrumentos de evaluación:** El control de estos estándares se llevará a cabo con el programa "Evalúa 2.00".

3.2.1. Representa personajes, situaciones, ideas y sentimientos... (rúbrica).

3.2.4. Trabaja en equipo para elaborar una pequeña representación grupal... (rúbrica)

3.4.3. Expone sus ideas de forma coherente y se expresa de forma correcta... (lista de control)

3.5.2. Demuestra autonomía y confianza en diferentes situaciones... (lista de control)

3.5.3. Participa en la recogida y organización de material... (registro anecdotario)

3.5.4. Acepta formar parte del grupo que le corresponda... (registro anecdotario).

Hecho este análisis de la sesión, a continuación, pasaremos a su desarrollo, el cual dividiremos en 3 partes:

1ª PARTE: ANIMACIÓN O PREPARACIÓN (10'-15')

La sesión comenzará en el aula de los alumnos, donde pasaremos lista, revisaremos que traen el material adecuado (chándal, bolsa de aseo, material necesario para las representaciones...) y explicaremos que en la sesión de hoy se realizarán las representaciones grupales, las cuales serán evaluadas por los propios compañeros (**coevaluación**). Esta evaluación se llevará a cabo por grupos y a partir de una ficha con diversos ítems aportada por el maestro de E.F. con preguntas como: ¿Os ha gustado la representación?, ¿Ha sido divertida? ¿Qué es lo que menos os ha gustado?, Pon nota del 1 al 10 a cada uno de los componentes del grupo, etc.

Posteriormente, seguiremos las rutinas diarias de ir en orden y silencio hasta la sala polivalente, donde los diferentes grupos comenzaran a preparar los materiales necesarios para su representación (decorado, disfraces, etc.).

2ª PARTE: PARTE PRINCIPAL (35'-40')

En esta parte comenzarán las representaciones, comenzarán en orden desde el grupo 1 al 5. Como ya dijimos, cada representación durará en torno a los 4-5 minutos. Tras cada representación el resto de grupos tendrá 1-2 minutos para rellenar la ficha evaluativa,

Por su parte, el maestro apoyará y reforzará los mensajes sobre la salud transmitidos por cada grupo tras sus representaciones. Así mismo, también evaluará los diferentes estándares de aprendizaje utilizando los instrumentos mencionados anteriormente.

3ª PARTE: PARTE FINAL (5'-10')

Terminamos la sesión con la recogida del material, el feed-back general sobre la sesión, comentarios de los alumnos/as y, finalmente, con las labores higiénicas. Por último, volvemos al aula en fila y en silencio.

CASO PRÁCTICO Nº6

El servicio de inspección (SIE) ha informado que una prioridad de todos los centros escolares para el curso próximo será:

"Mejorar el clima de convivencia y combatir el acoso escolar en los centros educativos".

Teniendo este objetivo presente, debemos elaborar una respuesta a nivel de centro y, más concretamente, nuestra actuación a través del área de Educación Física.

1. INTRODUCCIÓN

El contenido de este supuesto es muy importante dentro de nuestro **sistema educativo**, así como para la **EF,** pues trata aspectos fundamentales como la **convivencia escolar y la prevención del acoso o maltrato** entre iguales en los centros educativos. Concretamente, estos contenidos tienen un tratamiento más amplio en el **tema 25** de nuestro temario de E.F.

En los últimos meses estamos comprobando como ha aumentado considerablemente el número de casos de acoso escolar entre el alumnado de Primaria en los centros educativos. En muchos casos este acoso escolar siempre ha existido en nuestros centros, pero actualmente se dan más a conocer, las víctimas actúan y, en consecuencia, tanto los equipos directivos, los servicios de inspección y, en última instancia, los servicios sociales, toman las medidas correctivas necesarias ante esas conductas disruptivas que tanto daño pueden hacer a determinados alumnos/as.

Teniendo esto en cuenta, debemos partir de que la convivencia pacífica es la base sobre la que se construye cualquier estado democrático y de derecho. Nuestro sistema educativo, como formador de personas, no es ajeno a este hecho y lo incluye como una de las prioridades a conseguir por todos los centros escolares, incluyéndolo dentro de su **P.G.A.** y en sus **proyectos de actividades deportivas.** Para conseguir estas prioridades, a lo largo de todo el curso realizaremos una serie de tareas o actividades con el objetivo de transmitir y crear en nuestro alumnado una gran cantidad de valores y actitudes como el respeto, la solidaridad, el compañerismo... Estas actividades estarán incluidas en nuestro Proyecto Deportivo "Nuestro colegio se mueve".

Por otro lado, para comprender mejor el contenido de este supuesto analizaremos una serie de conceptos que se encuentran estrechamente relacionados con el enunciado.

En primer lugar, el **Servicio de Inspección** es considerado como un órgano externo al centro que realiza diversas funciones como valorar la adecuación de la infraestructura docente, evaluar las programaciones didácticas o dar información sobre las prioridades que deben cumplir y perseguir los centros educativos.

Por otro lado, dichas prioridades deben quedar recogidas en la **PGA,** que según la **Ley Orgánica 2/2006 (LOE)** es un documento propio y específico de cada centro educativo donde se recogen todos los objetivos y prioridades que se persiguen a lo largo de todo el curso escolar, así como las medidas o acciones para conseguirlos. Este documento concreta el **Proyecto Educativo** para cada curso escolar y garantiza el desarrollo coordinado de todas las actividades del centro.

Una de las prioridades que perseguimos es la **convivencia escolar,** definida por el **Ministerio de Educación** como "la coexistencia pacífica de los miembros de la comunidad educativa que permite el adecuado cumplimiento de los objetivos educativos en un clima que propicia el desarrollo integral de los estudiantes".

Otra de las prioridades es la **prevención del acoso escolar**, el cual se produce cuando un alumno/a se ve expuesto de forma repetida y durante un tiempo a diferentes formas de acoso u hostigamiento, por parte de un compañero/a o un grupo, quedando la víctima en situación de inferioridad respecto al agresor o agresores.

Por otro lado, según **Pieron** una **sesión** "es el punto de unión entre la programación, a veces muy teórica, y la realidad de la clase". Las sesiones las incluimos en **Unidades Didácticas,** que según **Jesús Viciana** son "la unidad mínima del currículum del alumno con pleno sentido en sí misma, aunque contiene unidades más pequeñas que son las sesiones".

También debemos destacar el concepto de **Proyecto Deportivo Escolar o programa de actividades deportivas,** el cual se define como el conjunto de actividades físicas y deportivas que se realizan en el centro educativo, en horario lectivo y no lectivo, con el fin de promover e inculcar un estilo de vida saludable a través del deporte.

Hecha esta introducción, seguiremos con el segundo apartado del supuesto.

2. MARCO LEGISLATIVO

El contenido de este supuesto queda perfectamente justificado mediante la legislación vigente para el curso 2016/17 en nuestra **comunidad de Madrid** a través de: **Ley Orgánica 8/2013 (LOMCE)**, **Ley Orgánica de Educación (LOE)**, el **Real Decreto 126/2014,** por el que se establece el **currículo básico de la Educación Primaria a nivel nacional**, y más concretamente el **Decreto 89/2014,** por el que se establece **el currículo de la Educación Primaria en la Comunidad de Madrid.**

Además, tendremos en cuenta otra como:

- ***Decreto 15/2007,*** *por el que se establece el marco regulador de la convivencia en los centros docentes de la Comunidad de Madrid.*

- **LEY 2/2010,** de **Autoridad del Profesor**.

- **Orden ECD65/2015** (relación de contenidos, criterios de evaluación y competencias)

- ***Orden 3622/2014,*** *por la que se regulan determinados aspectos de organización y funcionamiento, así como la evaluación y los documentos de aplicación en la Educación Primaria*

- ***Orden 1493/2015,*** *por la que se regula la evaluación y la promoción de los alumnos con necesidad específica de apoyo educativo.*

- ***Orden 11994/2012,*** *por la que se regula la jornada escolar en los centros docentes*

Teniendo en cuenta este marco legislativo, pasaremos a contextualizar este supuesto práctico.

3. CONTEXTUALIZACIÓN

El centro en el que se desarrollará las actividades de este supuesto está situado en la **Comunidad de Madrid** y cuenta con 499 alumnos. Cabe destacar que el centro cuenta con **jornada continua de 9 a 14 horas.**

El alumnado de Educación Primaria de nuestro centro presenta una edad que oscila entre los 6 y los 12 años. A nivel general, algunas de sus **características psicoevolutivas** más destacadas son: se encuentran en la edad de oro de los aprendizajes, presentan progresivamente una mayor independencia de los adultos y dependencia de sus amigos, van sistematizando hábitos higiénicos y de medidas de seguridad, van progresando en el respeto a las normas, los compañeros, los docentes, etc.

Dentro de estos alumnos/as encontramos varios ACNEAEs (alumnos/as que reciben una respuesta diferente a la ordinaria y requieren determinados apoyos y provisiones educativas) ante los cuales debemos adoptar medidas especiales según la actividad a realizar. Este tipo de alumnado será analizado en el apartado de atención a la diversidad.

Una vez analizado el contexto, pasaremos a analizar la intervención educativa del supuesto que se nos pide.

4. INTERVENCIÓN EDUCATIVA

4.1. RELACIÓN CON EL CURRÍCULUM

En primer lugar podemos destacar que la **LOMCE en su Disposición adicional cuarta** señala que: "Las administraciones educativas adoptarán medidas para que la **actividad física** y la **dieta equilibrada** formen parte del comportamiento infantil y juvenil. A estos efectos, promoverán la práctica diaria de **deporte y ejercicio** durante la jornada escolar...". De aquí se desprende la justificación o necesidad de elaboración de los proyectos deportivos en los centros escolares.

Por otro lado, con el trabajo del contenido de este supuesto se contribuye a la consecución de **diversos elementos curriculares** marcados en el **D.89/2014,** tales como el **Objetivo General de Etapa "m"**: *"Desarrollar sus capacidades afectivas en todos los ámbitos de la personalidad y en sus relaciones con los demás, así como una actitud contraria a la violencia, a los prejuicios de cualquier tipo y a los estereotipos sexistas"* y el **"k"**: *"Valorar la higiene y la salud, conocer y respetar el cuerpo humano, y utilizar la educación física y el deporte como medios para favorecer el desarrollo personal y social"*, o **las Competencias Clave Sociales y cívicas y** a través las interacciones sociales que se dan en los juegos y actividades, o **la competencia lingüística** mediante el uso del diálogo para la resolución de conflictos, entre otras.

También podemos destacar los **contenidos** establecidos en el **D.89/2014: "Valores del deporte", "Juego limpio" o "Valoración del deporte como herramienta para la resolución de situaciones conflictivas".** Así como el **Criterio de Evaluación nº9**: *"Opinar coherentemente con actitud crítica tanto desde la perspectiva de participante como de espectador, ante las posibles situaciones conflictivas surgidas, participando en debates, y aceptando las opiniones de los demás"* y los **estándares de aprendizaje evaluables: "9.3.** *Muestra buena disposición para solucionar los conflictos de manera razonable."* y **"9.4.** *Reconoce y califica* *negativamente las conductas inapropiadas que se producen en la práctica o en los espectáculos deportivos".*

4.2. METODOLOGÍA

En nuestra labor docente y a la hora de poner en práctica nuestras actividades deberemos procurar que el aprendizaje de nuestros alumnos/as sea significativo, con un carácter lúdico y global, mediante una enseñanza individualizada y atendiendo a la diversidad del alumnado.

Así mismo, también tendremos en cuenta lo establecido en la **Orden 65/2015 en su anexo II** que establece orientaciones para el trabajo por competencias en el aula y recomienda utilizar metodologías activas como del aprendizaje cooperativo, el aprendizaje por proyectos o el aprendizaje basado en problemas.

4.3. TEMPORALIZACIÓN Y RECURSOS

Las actividades y tareas relacionadas con el enunciado que nos pide este supuesto se encuentran incluidas en la **P.G.A.** y en el **Proyecto Deportivo** de nuestro centro, titulado "Nuestro colegio se mueve". Así mismo, se encuentran muy relacionadas con muchas de las Unidades Didácticas que incluye nuestra programación de E.F.

Por otro lado, para la correcta realización de cada actividad serán necesarios varios tipos de **recursos:**

- Humanos: Docentes, especialistas, voluntarios, los propios alumnos/as, las familias...

- Materiales: Los propios de E.F., los aportados por los voluntarios y especialistas, los propios materiales de los alumnos/as (ropa deportiva, bolsa de aseo...), etc.

- Instalaciones: Las propias del centro (aulas, pabellón, sala polivalente...), etc. Las cuales cumplen con la normativa establecida en el **RD 132/2010** de requisitos mínimos.

- Autorizaciones: Documento firmado por los padres donde se autorice a la realización de actividades fuera del centro y la utilización de la imagen de sus hijos en la página web del colegio, blog o revista escolar.

- TIC: El proyector y la pantalla digital para el visionado de videos y explicaciones, los Netbook de los alumnos/as para la realización de trabajos de investigación y práctica de juegos interactivos, etc.

4.4. INTERDISCIPLINARIEDAD Y ELEMENTOS TRANSVERSALES

Con este supuesto se puede plantear un **trabajo interdisciplinar** con todas las áreas del currículo de Educación Primaria establecido por el **D.89/2014**, por ejemplo, con **Lengua** en el establecimiento de las normas de aula o la elaboración de diálogos para la resolución de conflictos, o con **Educación Artística** para la realización de dibujos, pancartas, decoración del aula, etc.

Además, como ya se ha comentado, destacamos la inclusión de estas actividades en el **Proyecto Deportivo** que desarrolla nuestro centro *"El colegio se mueve"*, con actividades que analizaremos en un apartado posteriormente.

Por otro lado, siguiendo el **RD 126/2014,** a través de estas actividades trabajamos una serie de contenidos que pueden ser trabajados desde todas las áreas, conocidos como **elementos transversales,** principalmente con la *actividad física y la dieta equilibrada* o *educación para la prevención y resolución pacífica de conflictos*

4.5. ATENCIÓN A LA DIVERSIDAD

Para atender correctamente a todo el alumnado seguiremos lo marcado en la normativa que regula la atención personalizada del alumnado en nuestra comunidad a través de la **Orden 1493/2015,** destacando la **coordinación** necesaria con el equipo de orientación, jefatura de estudios, tutor, familias...

4.6. DESARROLLO DE LAS ACTIVIDADES

Como ya se ha comentado anteriormente, incluiremos en la **PGA** y en el Proyecto Deportivo Saludable aquellas actividades e intenciones que pretendemos desarrollar durante este curso. En este sentido, **todos los docentes** del centro podrán hacer sus aportaciones en las **reuniones de los equipos docentes**, las cuales se llevarán a **CCP** y, por último, aprobadas por el **claustro.**

En la PGA aparecen todas las acciones que realizará el centro durante el presente curso, las cuales van encaminadas a conseguir las siete **Competencias Clave** y los **Objetivos de la Educación Primaria** marcados en el **D.89/2014.**

Muchas de estas acciones o prioridades son recomendadas o establecidas por el Servicio de Inspección Educativa (SIE). Algunas de estas prioridades para este curso escolar son:

- Mejorar la salud del alumnado: alimentación, higiene...
- Respetar, cuidar y conservar el medio ambiente.
- Favorecer la creación de hábitos deportivos saludables.
- Mejorar el clima de convivencia escolar.
- Combatir el acoso escolar en los centros educativos.

A continuación, nos centraremos en estas dos últimas prioridades y describiremos algunas de las actividades a realizar a nivel de centro para intentar que se cumplan:

- **Plan de acción tutorial:** Elaboración de las Normas de aula al inicio de curso, charlas e informaciones sobre educación en valores (compañerismo, respeto a las normas etc.), sobre acoso escolar y ciberbulling, etc.

- **Difusión de normas de aula y normas de convivencia** en web del colegio, en los blog de cada curso...

- **Plan de formación del profesorado:** Realización de un grupo de trabajo o seminario para formar a los docentes del centro en la mejora de la convivencia y el acoso escolar.

- **Revisión del Plan de Convivencia del centro:** Se analizarán en las reuniones de equipo docente, en CCP y se aprobaran en claustro.

- **Comunicados a las familias (elaborados por el Equipo de Orientación):** A lo largo del curso se les darán diversos comunicados a las familias para que desde casa puedan trabajar y reforzar la convivencia y la prevención del acoso o maltrato entre iguales.

- **Plan de Lectura:** Se recomendarán libros y cuentos donde se fomente la convivencia, el compañerismo, la cooperación, el respeto, etc. En la biblioteca del centro habrá un listado con los libros recomendados. Participación en la elaboración del periódico escolar.

- **Celebración de días especiales:** Podemos destacar la celebración del día de la Paz o de la Interculturalidad (convivencia entre culturas), entre otros.

- **Decoración del aula, pasillos, etc.:** Se llevarán a cabo talleres donde se realizarán murales, posters, dibujos, etc., que serán colocados en los pasillos del centro y en el aula. También se trabajará desde el área de Educación Artística.

- **Creación de una Comisión de Convivencia Escolar** que se encargará de solucionar conflictos, informar y comprobar que se cumplen los objetivos previstos.

Es importante que al finalizar cada una de las actividades se elabore un **informe evaluativo** reflejando los aspectos positivos de las mismas, así como las que deben mejorarse de cara a futuras actividades similares. También se informará al claustro del desarrollo de las actividades y se darán los agradecimientos oportunos a los colaboradores y responsables. Estos informes los recogeremos en una memoria final del proyecto deportivo.

4.7. PROGRAMA DEPORTIVO DE CENTRO

Partiendo del **Decreto 89/2014** por la que se establecen las líneas generales para la elaboración del programa de actividades físicas y deportivas a realizar por los alumnos del centro, nuestro centro viene desarrollando durante el presente curso un **Proyecto Escolar Saludable,** el cual se compone de gran cantidad de actividades encaminadas a conseguir la formación integral y a la mejora de la calidad de vida y la salud de nuestros alumnos/as.

Entre los objetivos que pretendemos conseguir con nuestro Proyecto "Nuestro colegio se mueve" podemos destacar:

- Aumentar la práctica físico-deportiva diaria del alumnado.

- Educar en valores: participación, solidaridad, respeto...

- Aumentar el bagaje motriz de nuestros alumnos/as.

- Crear hábitos saludables (higienes, postura, alimentación...)

Dentro de este proyecto encontramos diversas actividades deportivas que se desarrollarán a lo largo del curso encaminadas a la mejora de la convivencia, la resolución de conflictos y evitar el acoso escolar, por ejemplo:

- **Los bailes por la paz:** Preparación de bailes y coreografías para representar durante el día de la paz.

- **Charlas y debates** sobre conductas negativas o inapropiadas en el deporte, sobre "fair-play" o juego limpio...

- **Los recreos deportivos:** Actividades lúdicas que se realizan durante el recreo, como la práctica de juegos populares, juegos y deportes alternativos, juegos de cooperación, etc.

- **Jornadas de Convivencia Escolar:** Durante el último trimestre se realizan unas jornadas de convivencia en un parque periurbano de la localidad donde participa todo el centro y se realizan diversas actividades y juegos donde lo fundamental es la cooperación y la colaboración.

- **Acampada final de curso:** Los alumnos/as de 6º de Primaria realizarán una excursión de dos días y una noche, donde se llevarán a cabo diversas actividades en el medio natural y dormirán al aire libre en tiendas de campaña.

4.8. ACTIVIDADES O IMPLICACIONES DESDE EL ÁREA DE E.F.

A continuación, señalaremos las aportaciones que se pueden realizar de forma específica desde el área de EF a la consecución de las prioridades de la PGA:

- **La UD nº1 "Empecemos el curso con buen pie"** se trabaja en todos los cursos e irá encaminada a la mejora de la convivencia entre los alumnos/as a través de juegos de cooperación, colaboración y participación de todos, donde el objetivo es la diversión y la mejora de la socialización.

Además, en esta primera UD se establece un debate para elaborar las normas de la clase de EF, así como las medidas a adoptar en caso de su incumplimiento.

- **UD de expresión corporal:** Realización de bailes y coreografías; representación de situaciones reales o inventadas sobre acoso, malas conductas en el deporte, etc.

- **UD de juegos populares:** Práctica de juegos populares que favorecen la convivencia intergeneracional. Válido para todos los cursos, no obstante, en los cursos elevados se puede incluir un pequeño trabajo de investigación.

- **Unidades didácticas de deportes adaptados:** Se pueden realizar diversas Unidades de deportes como fútbol, baloncesto, balonmano, etc., donde lo fundamental es fomentar el "fair-play" o juego limpio. Estarán dirigidas fundamentalmente para 5º y 6º.

- **UD de juegos y materiales alternativos:** A través de juegos con indiacas, fresbees, balones gigantes, paracaídas... en pequeño o gran grupo, podemos mejorar la participación y socialización de todos los alumnos/as. Este tipo de UD o sesiones se puede trabajar en todos los niveles.

- **UD de EF adaptada o especial:** A través de juegos de sensibilización para que todos los alumnos/as aprecien las dificultades que tienen sus compañeros/as ACNEAEs en la práctica de EF y en su vida diaria.

CASO PRÁCTICO Nº 7

Nuestro centro se encuentra desarrollando *"La semana del medio ambiente"*. Se debe plantear una sesión relacionada con dicho tema y proponer alguna actividad de nuestro *Programa Deportivo* que se pueda desarrollar durante esa semana.

1. INTRODUCCIÓN

El contenido de este supuesto es muy importante dentro de la E.F., pues trata sobre el medio ambiente y las actividades en el medio natural. Podemos destacar que estos aspectos tienen un tratamiento mucho más amplio en el **tema 15** del temario de oposición de E.F.

A través de "**La Semana del Medio Ambiente"** trataremos de inculcar en nuestros/as alumnos/as una serie de actitudes y valores sobre su conservación, así como hábitos de su cuidado y protección a través de actividades físicas. Así mismo, trataremos de transmitirles el gran bagaje y patrimonio que tienen en sus manos para generaciones venideras. Todo ello a través de actividades que se celebraran durante esta semana, las cuales están incluidas en la **PGA y el Programa Deportivo** de nuestro centro *"Nuestro colegio se mueve"*.

Por otro lado, para comprender mejor el contenido de este supuesto analizaremos una serie de conceptos que se encuentran estrechamente relacionados con su enunciado.

En primer lugar, la **PGA** es un documento propio y específico de cada centro educativo donde se recogen los objetivos que se persiguen en el curso actual, así como las medidas o acciones para conseguirlos.

También debemos destacar el concepto de **Programa o Proyecto Deportivo Escolar,** el cual se define como el conjunto de actividades físicas y deportivas que se realizan en el centro educativo, en horario lectivo y no lectivo, con el fin de promover e inculcar un estilo de vida saludable a través del deporte.

Por otro lado, según **Pieron** una **sesión** "es el punto de unión entre la programación, a veces muy teórica, y la realidad de la clase". Las sesiones las incluimos en **Unidades Didácticas,** que según **Jesús Viciana** son "la unidad mínima del currículum del alumno con pleno sentido en sí misma, aunque contiene unidades más pequeñas que son las sesiones".

Por último, el supuesto gira en torno al concepto **"actividades físicas en el medio natural",** que se define como, según **Bernardette,** "los desplazamientos individuales o colectivos hacia un fin más o menos próximo utilizando o luchando con los elementos del entorno físico".

Hecha esta breve introducción pasaremos a analizar el segundo apartado de este supuesto.

2. MARCO LEGISLATIVO

La contenido de este supuesto queda perfectamente justificado mediante la legislación vigente para el curso 2016/17 en nuestra comunidad de Castilla-La Mancha a través de: **Ley Orgánica 8/2013 (LOMCE)**, **Ley Orgánica de Educación (LOE)**, la **Ley 7/2010, de Educación de Castilla-La Mancha**, el **Real Decreto 126/2014,** por el que se establece el **currículo básico de la Educación Primaria a nivel nacional**, y más concretamente el **Decreto 54/2014,** por el que se establece **el currículo de la Educación Primaria en CLM.**

Además, tendremos en cuenta otra normativa como:

- **D.66/2013** de atención a la diversidad en CLM
- **Orden 5/08/2014** de organización y evaluación de Primaria en CLM
- **Resolución 11/03/15** (categorización y ponderación de estándares)
- **Orden ECD65/2015** (relación de contenidos, criterios de evaluación y competencias)

Teniendo en cuenta este marco legislativo, pasaremos a contextualizar este supuesto práctico.

3. CONTEXTUALIZACIÓN

El centro en el que se desarrollará estas actividades está situado en la Comunidad de Castilla-La Mancha y cuenta con 499 alumnos.

A pesar de que muchas de las actividades de "La Semana del Medio Ambiente" se llevarán a cabo con alumnos y alumnas de todos los niveles, la sesión que se nos pide la realizaremos con alumnos/as de **5º de Primaria**, concretamente con el grupo 5ºA, formado por 25 alumnos, 11 chicas y 14 chicos. En general, todos los alumnos/as participan activamente en clase.

Estos alumnos se encuentran en un intervalo de edad que oscila entre los 10 y 11 años. Algunas de sus **características psicoevolutivas** más destacadas son:

A nivel cognitivo: Se sitúan en el estadio de las operaciones formales de Piaget, lo que les permite realizar operaciones mentales abstractas.

A nivel socio-afectivo: Empiezan progresivamente a independizarse de los adultos, aumentando su autonomía y afianzando su personalidad.

A nivel motriz: Comienzan los procesos característicos de la pubertad (crecimiento, aumento de musculatura, etc.). Consolidad su esquema corporal y toman conciencia global de su cuerpo, sistematizan hábitos higiénicos y respetan las medidas de seguridad.

Una vez analizado el contexto, pasaremos a analizar la intervención educativa del supuesto que se nos pide.

4. INTERVENCIÓN EDUCATIVA

4.1. RELACIÓN CON EL CURRÍCULUM

En primer lugar, podemos destacar que la **LOMCE en su Disposición adicional cuarta** señala que: "Las administraciones educativas adoptarán medidas para que la **actividad física** y la **dieta equilibrada** formen parte del comportamiento infantil y juvenil. A estos efectos, promoverán la práctica diaria de **deporte y ejercicio** durante la jornada escolar...". De aquí se desprende la justificación o necesidad de elaboración de proyectos deportivos en los centros.

Por otro lado, con el trabajo del contenido de este supuesto se contribuye a la consecución de **diversos elementos curriculares** marcados en el **D.54/2014**, tales como el **Objetivo General de Etapa "k":** "*"Valorar la higiene y la salud, aceptar el propio cuerpo y el de los otros, respetar las diferencias y utilizar la educación física y el deporte como medios para favorecer el desarrollo personal y social", o* **las Competencias Clave Sociales y cívicas y** a través las interacciones sociales que se dan en los juegos y actividades, o **Conciencia y expresiones culturales**, a través de conservación y mejora del medio natural.

También podemos destacar el **Bloque de Contenidos nº2 "Juegos y deportes"** que se trabaja en 5º y 6º de Primaria, con contenidos como: "realización de actividades físicas en el medio natural" o "conservación del entorno físico".

Así mismo, podemos destacar el **Criterio de Evaluación nº6** que se trabaja en 5º de Primaria en este mismo bloque: "Participar de manera activa en actividades físicas en el medio natural", y su **estándar de aprendizaje evaluable 2.6.2.** "Respeta el medio natural en la práctica de actividades físicas y deportivas", entre otros.

4.2. METODOLOGÍA

En nuestra labor docente y a la hora de poner en práctica nuestras actividades deberemos tener en cuenta las **orientaciones metodológicas** marcadas en el **D.54/2014** y procurar que el aprendizaje de nuestros alumnos/as sea significativo, con un carácter lúdico y global, mediante una enseñanza individualizada y atendiendo a la diversidad del alumnado.

Así mismo, también tendremos en cuenta lo establecido en la **Orden 65/2015 en su anexo II** que establece orientaciones para el trabajo por competencias en el aula y recomienda utilizar metodologías activas como del aprendizaje cooperativo, el aprendizaje por proyectos o el aprendizaje basado en problemas.

4.3. TEMPORALIZACIÓN Y RECURSOS

Las actividades y tareas que nos pide este supuesto se encuentran incluidas en la **P.G.A.** y en el **Proyecto Deportivo** de nuestro centro, titulado "Nuestro colegio se mueve", las cuales se desarrollarán durante el **tercer trimestre** con la llegada del buen tiempo y de la primavera. Así mismo, la sesión que se nos pide forma parte de la **U.D. nº11** de nuestra programación de E.F. **"Me oriento en la naturaleza",** que a su vez se encuentra estrechamente relacionada con "La Semana del Medio Ambiente".

Por otro lado, para la correcta realización de cada actividad serán necesarios varios tipos de **recursos:**

- Humanos: Docentes, especialistas, voluntarios, los propios alumnos/as, etc.

- Materiales: Materiales propios del centro y de E.F., los aportados por los voluntarios y especialistas (fichas, mapas...), los propios materiales de los alumnos/as (ropa deportiva, bolsa de aseo...), etc.

- Instalaciones: Las propias del centro que cumplen con la normativa establecida en el **RD 132/2010** de requisitos mínimos (aulas, patio, huerto escolar...), Jardín botánico, parque periurbano la pulgosa, etc.

- Autorizaciones: Documento firmado por los padres o tutores donde se recojan el consentimiento para la salida del centro.

- TIC: El proyector y la pantalla digital para el visionado de videos y explicaciones, los Netbook de los alumnos/as para la realización de trabajos de investigación y práctica de juegos interactivos, etc.

4.4. INTERDISCIPLINARIEDAD Y ELEMENTOS TRANSVERSALES

Con este supuesto se puede plantear un **trabajo interdisciplinar** con otras áreas, por ejemplo, con **Ciencias Naturales** a través del reciclaje y del cuidado del medio ambiente o con **Educación Artística** para la realización de dibujos, pancartas, decoración del aula, etc.

Además, como ya se ha comentado, destacamos la inclusión de estas actividades en el **Proyecto Deportivo** de nuestro centro, con actividades que analizaremos en un apartado posteriormente.

Por otro lado, siguiendo el **RD 126/2014,** a través de estas actividades trabajamos una serie de contenidos que pueden ser trabajados desde todas las áreas, conocidos como **elementos transversales,** principalmente con la actividad física y la dieta equilibrada o educación por el desarrollo sostenible y el cuidado del medio.

4.5. ATENCIÓN A LA DIVERSIDAD

En este apartado debemos tener en cuenta lo establecido en el **Decreto 66/2013** que regula la respuesta a la diversidad del alumnado en CLM, en las medidas de atención a la diversidad establecidas en la PGA y en la programación de E.F.

En este caso no encontramos ningún alumno/a con características especiales a destacar, si bien debemos estar preparados por si en algún momento algún alumno/a necesitase de una atención más especializada. Para ello será necesario un contacto y un trabajo coordinado y continuo con los especialistas correspondientes, tutores y familias.

4.6. PROGRAMA DEPORTIVO DE CENTRO

Partiendo de la **Orden de 03/10/2016** por la que se crea y organiza la **Red de Centros Docentes Saludables de CLM,** nuestro centro viene desarrollando durante el presente curso un **Proyectos Escolar Saludable** llamado *"Nuestro colegio se mueve"***,** el cual se compone de gran cantidad de actividades encaminadas a conseguir la formación integral y a la mejora de la calidad de vida y la salud de nuestros alumnos/as, y donde **participa todo el claustro** tras su **aprobación e inclusión en la PGA.**

Entre los objetivos que pretendemos conseguir con nuestro Proyecto "Nuestro colegio se mueve" podemos destacar:

- Aumentar la práctica físico-deportiva diaria del alumnado.

- Educar en valores: participación, solidaridad, respeto...

- Aumentar el bagaje motriz de nuestros alumnos/as.

- Crear hábitos saludables (higienes, postura, alimentación...)

Dentro de este proyecto encontramos diversas actividades deportivas y culturales que se desarrollarán a lo largo de esta semana tan especial, entre otras podemos destacar las siguientes:

- Visita al parque botánico.

- Carrera de Orientación en el parque periurbano "La Pulgosa"

- Nuestro huerto escolar.

- Aprendemos a reciclar

- Las TIC y la Naturaleza

4.7. DESARROLLO DE LAS ACTIVIDADES

De la gran cantidad y variedad de actividades que se realizarán en nuestro centro durante "La Semana del Medio Ambiente", a continuación, desarrollaremos una de ellas, como así nos lo pide el enunciado del supuesto.

- VISITA AL PARQUE BOTÁNICO.

En primer lugar, esta actividad ha sido aprobada por el claustro e incluida en la PGA y en nuestro proyecto deportivo. La realizarán los alumnos/as de 5º y 6º de Primaria y colaborarán los tutores de dichos cursos y algunos especialistas, como el de inglés y el de E.F.

El traslado hasta el jardín botánico se realizará a pie, ya que se encuentra unos 2 km de nuestro centro, por lo que los docentes prestarán especial atención a los cruces de calles y al respeto de los alumnos/as por los elementos de la ciudad, de tal forma que reforzaremos los valores cívicos en ellos.

Se mandará previamente un comunicado a las familias donde se indique el día de realización de la actividad y el material que deben aportar: mochila con agua y almuerzo, gorra, etc.

La actividad durará en torno a las 3 horas, de 10 de la mañana hasta las 13:00, con descanso intermedio para almorzar y recuperar energía. La salida del centro será alrededor de las 9:15 y su regreso a las 14:00.

Una vez en las instalaciones del "Jardín Botánico" los alumnos/as se dividirán en grupos y participarán en varios talleres preparados y desarrollados por los monitores del propio jardín.

Al finalizar la actividad se realizará un **informe evaluativo** reflejando los aspectos positivos de la misma, así como las que deben mejorarse de cara a futuras actividades similares. También se informará al claustro del desarrollo de la actividad y se darán los agradecimientos oportunos a los colaboradores y responsables. Estos informes los recogeremos en una memoria final de nuestro proyecto.

4.8. DESARROLLO DE UNA SESIÓN

La sesión que a continuación desarrollaremos se encuentra incluida dentro de la UD "Me oriento en la Naturaleza". Esta sesión es la última de la UD, es la número 7, y sirve como colofón final a las jornadas ambientales y de orientación celebradas en la escuela.

Esta sesión se realizará en el parque periurbano "La Pulgosa" con la colaboración de un grupo de expertos en orientación, los cuales ya nos dieron una charla teórico-práctica en nuestro centro. Estos monitores aportarán todo el material necesario para la realización de la sesión: mapas, brújulas, etc.

Previamente a la sesión tendremos en cuenta que el traslado de los alumnos/as se realizará en autobús y entregaremos a las familias un comunicado con la información sobre la actividad.

A continuación, analizaremos algunos aspectos a tener en cuenta de esta sesión:

- **Duración**: Aproximadamente 1 hora

- **Instalación**: Parque "La Pulgosa"

- **Material:** Los aportados por los alumnos/as (mochila, gorra...), el aportado por los colaboradores (balizas, mapas, brújula...)

- **Contenidos:** *"Realización de actividades físicas en el medio natural", "conservación del medio ambiente", "actividades lúdicas en el medio natural", "participación en equipo".*

- **Objetivos didácticos:**

- Participar en actividades físicas y deportivas en el medio natural

- Respetar el medio natural en la práctica de actividades físicas

- Responsabilizar de la eliminación de residuos que se generan en el medio natural

- Mostrar autonomía y confianza en diferentes situaciones

- Incorporar en sus rutinas el cuidado e higiene corporal

- Aceptar formar parte del grupo y el resultado de las competiciones con deportividad

- Manifestar una actitud de respeto hacia el docente y sus decisiones

- **Metodología:** Resolución de problemas y descubrimiento guiado

- **Competencias Clave**: Sociales y Cívicas, Conciencia y expresiones culturales

- **Evaluación: Estándares de aprendizaje e instrumentos de evaluación:** El control de estos estándares se llevará a cabo con el programa "Evalúa 2.00".

2.6.1. Participa en actividades físicas y deportivas en el medio natural (lista de control)

2.6.2. Respeta el medio natural en la práctica de actividades físicas (lista de control)

2.6.3. Se hace responsable de la eliminación de residuos que se generan en el medio natural (lista de control)

2.8.2. Muestra autonomía y confianza en diferentes situaciones (lista de control)

2.8.3. Incorpora en sus rutinas el cuidado e higiene corporal (registro anecdotario)

2.8.5. Acepta formar parte del grupo y el resultado de las competiciones con deportividad (registro anecdotario).

2.8.6. Manifiesta una actitud de respeto hacia el docente y sus decisiones (registro)

Hecho este análisis, a continuación, pasaremos al desarrollo de la sesión:

1ª PARTE: ANIMACIÓN (10'-15')

Se realiza una primera toma de contacto y una breve charla de los monitores sobre la actividad. Después se divide la clase en grupos de 2-3 alumnos/as y se reparte un mapa y una brújula por grupo.

2ª PARTE: PARTE PRINCIPAL (35'-40')

Se lleva a cabo la actividad de orientación para encontrar las balizas que los monitores han establecido a lo largo del parque.

Las salidas de los grupos se realizan cada 2 minutos y en orden inverso, es decir, un grupo busca las balizas del 1 al 10 y el siguiente del 10 al 1.

Cuando los alumnos/as terminan el recorrido vuelven a la zona de salida para comprobar si ha sido bien realizado o no.

3ª PARTE: PARTE FINAL (5'-10')

En esta última parte comprobamos los resultados, ponemos en común la experiencia y utilizamos las instalaciones del parque para realizar las labores de higiene personal.

NOTAS ACLARATORIAS A LA SESIÓN:

La labor del maestro a lo largo de la sesión será la de motivar y ayudar a aquellos alumnos/as que lo soliciten o anden más despistados.

Además, tomará notas para la elaboración del informe evaluativo de la actividad que se incluirá en la memoria del proyecto deportivo.

CASO PRÁCTICO Nº8

Describe 2 sesiones sobre la iniciación de un deporte colectivo para un grupo de 22 alumnos/as. En dicho grupo se encuentra un alumno que suele insultar y molestar a dos niñas de otro grupo y un alumno con TDAH.

1. INTRODUCCIÓN

Actualmente, el **deporte** se ha convertido en uno de los grandes fenómenos sociales y culturales del momento. La escuela no es ajena a este hecho e incluye las actividades deportivas como un contenido más a desarrollar por la E.F. en Primaria en busca del desarrollo global del alumnado.

Concretamente la **iniciación deportiva** se trata en los dos últimos cursos de primaria, y de forma más específica en el **Tema 14** de nuestro temario de oposición.

Por otro lado, para entender mejor el contenido de este supuesto analizaremos de una serie de conceptos inherentes al enunciado del mismo.

En primer lugar, **Pieron** define **sesión** como "el punto de unión entre la programación, a veces muy teórica, y la realidad de la clase". Pero las sesiones no son elementos aislados, se incluyen en **Unidades Didácticas, las cuales Jesús Viciana** las define como "la unidad mínima del currículum del alumno con pleno sentido en sí misma".

Por otro lado, **Parlebas** define **deporte colectivo** como "aquellos en los que se participa en equipo para conseguir un mismo objetivo, realizando operaciones de colaboración y cooperación de todos, tratando de superar la oposición de los contrarios que persiguen el mismo objetivo".

Por último, en el supuesto encontramos un alumno **ACNEAE,** que según el **Decreto 66/2013** "son aquellos que reciben una respuesta educativa diferente a la ordinaria y que requieren determinados apoyos y provisiones educativas, por un periodo de escolarización o a lo largo de toda ella." Concretamente el supuesto presenta un **TDAH,** que según **Taylor** se caracteriza por ser niños desorganizados, inquietos, impulsivos y que se distraen con facilidad.

Hecha esta breve introducción pasaremos a analizar el segundo apartado de este supuesto.

2. MARCO LEGISLATIVO

La sesiones que se nos piden, así como la U.D. en la que se enmarca, queda perfectamente justificada mediante la legislación vigente para el curso 2016/17 en nuestra comunidad de CLM a través de: **Ley Orgánica 8/2013 (LOMCE)**, **Ley Orgánica de Educación (LOE)**, la **Ley 7/2010, de Educación de Castilla-La Mancha**, el **Real Decreto 126/2014,** por el que se establece el **currículo básico de la Educación Primaria a nivel nacional**, y más concretamente el **Decreto 54/2014,** por el que se establece **el currículo de la Educación Primaria en CLM.**

Además, tendremos en cuenta otra como:

- **D.66/2013** de atención a la diversidad en CLM

- **Orden 5/08/2014** de organización y evaluación de Primaria en CLM

- **Resolución 11/03/15** (categorización y ponderación de estándares)

- **Orden ECD65/2015** (relación de contenidos, criterios de evaluación y competencias)

- **Decreto 3/2008** de convivencia escolar en CLM.

Teniendo en cuenta este marco legislativo, pasaremos a contextualizar este supuesto práctico.

3. CONTEXTUALIZACIÓN

El centro en el que se desarrollará la sesión está situado en Castilla-La Mancha y cuenta con 499 alumnos. Esta sesión se impartirá en el grupo **5ºA**, formado por **22 alumnos, 11 chicos y 11 chicas.**

Estos alumnos se encuentran en un intervalo de edad que oscila entre los 10 y los 11 años. Algunas de sus **características psicoevolutivas** más destacadas a **nivel cognitivo, socio-afectivo y motriz** son: Se sitúan en el estadio de las operaciones formales de Piaget, empiezan a independizarse de los adultos, comienzan los procesos de la pubertad, consolidad su esquema corporal, etc.

Dentro del grupo encontramos dos alumnos con unas características "especiales":

- **Un alumno que suele humillar e insultar a dos niñas de otro grupo:** Siguiendo la **Resolución 20/01/2006** de maltrato entre iguales, este alumno tiene abierto un **protocolo de maltrato escolar** por parte del equipo directivo, informando tanto a la familia como a inspección y servicios sociales de tales hechos. En nuestras clases prestaremos especial atención a su comportamiento, lo motivaremos, le reforzaremos las conductas positivas, mantendremos conversaciones con él y, en caso de que sea necesario, aplicaremos las medidas correctoras correspondientes según las **NCOF** de nuestro centro y el **Decreto 3/2008** de convivencia escolar.

- **Un alumno con TDHA:** Este alumno se encuentra medicado, por lo que puede realizar las actividades y participar en clase de forma normalizada. No obstante, durante las sesiones prestaremos especial atención a su socialización, comportamiento, posibles distracciones, etc.

Una vez analizado el contexto, pasaremos a analizar la intervención educativa del supuesto que se nos pide.

4. INTERVENCIÓN EDUCATIVA

4.1. RELACIÓN CON EL CURRÍCULUM

Con el trabajo de esta sesión contribuiremos a conseguir **diversos elementos curriculares** marcados en el **D.54/2014**, tales como el **Objetivo General de Etapa "k":** *""Valorar la higiene y la salud, aceptar el propio cuerpo y el de los otros, respetar las diferencias y…".* Así como **las Competencias Clave Sociales y cívicas y Aprender a Aprender,** mediante las interacciones sociales que se dan en los juegos y actividades y con el conocimiento de uno mismo.

También podemos destacar el **Bloque de Contenidos nº2** que se trabaja en 5º y 6º de Primaria **"Juegos y Deportes"** y el **contenido** "Tipos de juegos y actividades deportivas"**,** entre otros. Así mismo, también destacamos el **Criterio de Evaluación nº4** para 5º curso: *"Conocer y valorar la diversidad de actividades físicas, lúdicas, recreativas y artísticas",* y el **estándar de aprendizaje evaluable 2.4.1.** *"Expone las diferencias, características y/o relaciones entre juegos populares, deportes colectivos..."***,** entre otros.

4.2. METODOLOGÍA

En nuestra labor docente y a la hora de poner en práctica nuestras sesiones, deberemos tener en cuenta lo marcado en el **D.54/2014** (aprendizaje significativo, carácter lúdico y global, enseñanza individualizada, etc.) y en la **Orden 65/2015 en su anexo II** y utilizar metodologías activas como el aprendizaje cooperativo, el aprendizaje por proyectos o el aprendizaje basado en problemas.

En este sentido, los **estilos de enseñanza** que utilizaremos serán fundamentalmente la resolución de problemas, el descubrimiento guiado y la asignación de tareas.

4.3. TEMPORALIZACIÓN Y RECURSOS

Las sesiones que a continuación desarrollamos se enmarcan dentro de la **UD número 9** de nuestra programación y se titula **"Me gusta el fútbol",** la cual consta de **8 sesiones** que se desarrollan en el **tercer trimestre.**

(si da tiempo se mete la temporalización)

En relación con los **recursos** que utilizaremos en estas sesiones destacamos son un pabellón cubierto y una pista polideportiva al aire libre, los cuales cumplen con la normativa establecida en el **RD 132/2010.** Además del **material** suficiente y necesario, por ejemplo, pelotas, balones de fútbol, petos, etc.

También destacamos el **uso de las TIC,** como el uso del proyector y la pantalla digital para el visionado de videos y explicaciones, y los Netbook de los alumnos/as para la realización de un trabajo de investigación.

4.4. INTERDISCIPLINARIEDAD Y ELEMENTOS TRANSVERSALES

A través de estas sesiones se puede plantear un **trabajo interdisciplinar** con otras áreas como **Lengua,** para la realización de trabajos escritos o **Ciencias Naturales** con en el conocimiento de pautas saludables. Así como desarrollar los **elementos transversales,** como por ejemplo Educación Cívica o Educación para la actividad física y la dieta equilibrada.

Además, estas sesiones se encuentra estrechamente relacionada con el **Proyecto Deportivo** que desarrolla nuestro centro *"El colegio se mueve"* con actividades como "Los recreos deportivos" o "Las competiciones de fin de trimestre".

4.5. EVALUACIÓN

Según la **Orden 5/08/2014**, la **evaluación de nuestro alumnado será continua**, siendo evaluados a través de diferentes estándares de aprendizaje.

Se utilizarán diferentes **instrumentos de evaluación** como el registro anecdotario, las listas de control y el portfolio. Además, utilizaremos la herramienta evaluativa **"Evalúa 2.00",** la cual, siguiendo la **Resolución**

11/03/15, categoriza los estándares en: Básicos (50%), Intermedios (40%) y Avanzados (10%), en nuestro centro.

Cabe destacar que la evaluación se llevará a cabo tanto con los alumnos, como con el proceso de enseñanza y la propia práctica docente.

4.6. DESARROLLO DE LA SESIÓN

A continuación, desarrollaremos las **sesiones nº6 y nº8** de la U.D. *"Me gusta el fútbol"*, dedicadas al trabajo de iniciación deportiva de este deporte colectivo.

4.6.1. SESIÓN 1

La sesión número 6 de esta U.D. se centra en el desarrollo de mini-partidillos de fútbol mediante la utilización de materiales diferentes a los típicos balones de fútbol.

En primer lugar, analizaremos algunos aspectos a tener en cuenta:

- **Título**: ¿Con qué jugamos hoy?

- **Duración**: 1 hora

- **Instalación**: Pabellón

- **Material:** Balón de playa, balón de rugby, conos, petos, etc.

- **Contenidos:** "Adaptación de la ejecución de las habilidades motrices", "estrategias de cooperación y oposición", "deportes colectivos", "higiene personal".

- **Objetivos didácticos:**

- Adaptar las habilidades motrices de manipulación de objetos...

- Realizar actividades físicas y juegos adaptando las habilidades motrices".

- Realizar combinaciones de las habilidades motrices...

- Incorporar en sus rutinas el cuidado e higiene del cuerpo.

- **Metodología:** Asignación de tareas y resolución de problemas.

- **Competencias Clave**: Sociales y Cívicas, Aprender a aprender

- **Evaluación: Estándares de aprendizaje e instrumentos:**

2.1.3. "Adapta las habilidades motrices de manipulación de objetos..." (lista de control).

2.1.6. "Realiza actividades físicas y juegos adaptando las habilidades motrices" (lista de control)

2.2.2. "Realiza combinaciones de las habilidades motrices..." (lista de control).

1.8.3. "Incorpora en sus rutinas el cuidado e higiene del cuerpo" (registro)

Hecho este análisis de la sesión, a continuación, pasaremos a su desarrollo, el cual dividiremos en 3 partes:

1ª PARTE: ANIMACIÓN Y CALENTAMIENTO (10'-15')

La sesión comenzará en el aula de los alumnos, donde pasaremos lista, revisaremos que traen el material adecuado (chándal y bolsa de aseo), se nombran los encargados, explicaremos brevemente el contenido de la sesión Después, los alumnos/as se dirigen en orden hacia la pista polideportiva, donde realizarán un breve calentamiento articular en el centro de la pista, mientras el maestro y los encargados llegan con los materiales.

Posteriormente, realizaremos el juego: "Haz lo que yo digo": El maestro irá indicando una serie de acciones que los alumnos/as deberán realizar, por ejemplo: tocar una canasta, una portería, subir y bajar las escaleras del patio, desplazarse en cuadrupedia, hacer grupos de 3, de 4, de 6... La última indicación será hacer grupos de 4, que nos servirán para la parte principal. De este modo formaremos 4 grupos de 4 y 2 de 3 alumnos/as.

2ª PARTE: PARTE PRINCIPAL (35'-40')

En esta parte los alumnos/as realizarán mini-partidillos de 3-4 contra 3-4 utilizando diferentes materiales. Para ello dividiremos la pista polideportiva en tres partes. Cada parte tendrá 2 porterías realizadas con conos, de 1 metro aproximadamente. Además, cada parte se dividirá en otras 2 mitades. En cada mitad se ubicará cada grupo. Estos grupos, a la señal del maestro, irán girando en el sentido de las agujas del reloj hacia la mitad de campo inmediatamente siguiente a la que se encontraban. Se jugará sin portero, por lo que ningún alumno/a podrá coger el balón con las manos.

En la parte 1 se jugará con balón de playa, en la 2 con pelota gigante y en la 3 con balón de rugby.

3ª PARTE: PARTE FINAL Y VUELTA A LA CALMA (5'-10')

En esta parte realizamos unos ejercicios de relajación a través de ejercicios de flexibilidad de forma individual. Terminamos la sesión con la recogida del material y el cumplimiento del objetivo higiénico. Por último, volverán a su aula en fila y en silencio.

Durante esta última parte aprovecharemos para realizar algunas reflexiones finales sobre la sesión, realizar las anotaciones pertinentes en nuestro cuaderno y anticipar el contenido de la próxima sesión (para motivar).

OBSERVACIONES: En todo momento prestaremos especial atención al alumno con TDAH para que participe con normalidad en los partidos, así como con el alumno con el protocolo abierto con el fin de que no se muestre agresivo con sus compañeros/as.

4.6.2. SESIÓN 2

En este apartado desarrollaremos la sesión nº 8 de esta U.D. en la cual recogeremos los trabajos teóricos individuales que se les pidió en la primera sesión sobre contenidos de la U.D. y se les pasará una prueba práctica que se evaluará mediante una rúbrica.

Podemos destacar los siguientes elementos:

- **Título**: "Demuestra lo que sabes"

- **Duración**: 1 hora

- **Instalación**: Pista polideportiva

- **Material:** Petos, balones de fútbol, conos, etc.

- **Contenidos: "Uso de las TIC",** "estrategias de cooperación y oposición", "adaptación de las habilidades motrices", "higiene personal".

- **Objetivos didácticos:**

- "Adaptar las habilidades motrices de manipulación de objetos…"

- "Utilizar las nuevas tecnologías para localizar y extraer información"

- "Presentar sus trabajos atendiendo a unas pautas establecida"

- "Exponer sus ideas de forma coherente y se expresa de forma correcta"

- **Metodología:** Asignación de tareas y resolución de problemas.

- **Competencias Clave**: Sociales y Cívicas, Aprender a aprender

- **Evaluación: Estándares de aprendizaje e instrumentos:**

2.1.3. "Adapta las habilidades motrices de manipulación de objetos…" (rúbrica)

2.7.1. "Utiliza las nuevas tecnologías para localizar y extraer información" (portfolio)

2.7.2. "Presenta sus trabajos atendiendo a unas pautas establecida" (portfolio)

2.7.3. "Expone sus ideas de forma coherente y se expresa de forma correcta" (portfolio)

A continuación, desarrollaremos la sesión en 3 partes:

1ª PARTE: ANIMACIÓN Y CALENTAMIENTO (10'-15')

Seguiremos la rutina marcada en las sesiones anteriores. Además, en el aula recogeremos los **trabajos teóricos** individuales comentados anteriormente.

Una vez en la pista polideportiva repartiremos petos de 4 colores, con el objetivo de formar 4 equipos de 5 o 6 componentes, los cuales nos servirán para el primer juego y para la parte principal de la sesión.

Como juego de animación realizaremos "Polis y cacos", donde los alumnos/as con peto rojo y verde harán de "polis" y los de peto azul y amarillo de "cacos". Después cambiarán de roles.

2ª PARTE: PARTE PRINCIPAL (35'-40')

En esta parte realizaremos 2 actividades. Por un lado, el maestro pasará la prueba práctica de 2 en 2 alumnos/as. Y, por otro, los demás alumnos/as estarán realizando partidillos de 5-6 contra 5-6.

Cada mini partidillo se realizará en media pista polideportiva. Las porterías se realizarán con conos y se situarán en los laterales de la pista. En esta ocasión si habrá portero y se procurará que todos jueguen contra todos.

En un espacio asfaltado anexo a la pista se encontrará el maestro pasando y evaluando la prueba práctica, la cual consistirá en:

- Zig-zag entre conos (conducción)
- Pases y recepciones
- Tiro a portería (hecha con conos)

Los niveles de logro de la **rúbrica** irán del 1 al 5, siendo 1 como "no aceptable" y el 5 "excelente".

A los alumnos/as se les irá llamando de 2 en 2, siendo estos siempre de equipos distintos con el fin de no desnivelar los equipos.

3ª PARTE: PARTE FINAL Y VUELTA A LA CALMA (5'-10')

Para terminar la sesión, los alumnos/as realizarán una o varias tandas de penaltis (según el tiempo disponible). Terminamos la sesión con la recogida del material, el feed-back sobre la sesión y las labores higiénicas. Por último, volverán a su aula en fila y en silencio.

BIBLIOGRAFÍA

- Álvarez Del Villar, C. (1987). La preparación física del fútbol basada en el atletismo. Madrid: Gymnos.
- Blanco, T. (1991). Para jugar como jugábamos. Salamanca: Ed. Serie Abierta.
- Blázquez Sánchez, D. (1992). Evaluar en E.F. Barcelona: INDE.
- Blázquez Sánchez, D. y otros, (1995). La iniciación deportiva y el deporte escolar. Barcelona: INDE.
- Blázquez Sánchez, D. (2010). Enseñar por competencias en E.F. Barcelona: INDE.
- Consejería de Educación, Juventud y Deporte de la Comunidad de Madrid (2007). Decreto 15/2007, por el que se establece el marco regulador de la convivencia en los centros docentes de la Comunidad de Madrid. Madrid.
- Consejería de Educación, Juventud y Deporte de la Comunidad de Madrid (2010). LEY 2/2010, de Autoridad del Profesor. Madrid.
- Consejería de Educación, Juventud y Deporte de la Comunidad de Madrid (2014). Decreto 89/2014, por el que se establece el currículo de la Educación Primaria en la Comunidad Autónoma de Madrid. Madrid.
- Consejería de Educación, Juventud y Deporte de la Comunidad de Madrid (2015). Orden 1493/2015, por la que se regula la evaluación y la promoción de los alumnos con necesidad específica de apoyo educativo. Madrid.
- Consejería de Educación, Juventud y Deporte de la Comunidad de Madrid (2014). *Orden 3622/2014, por la que se regulan determinados aspectos de organización y funcionamiento, así como la evaluación y los documentos de aplicación en la Educación Primaria.* Madrid
- Contreras Jordan, O.R. (1998). Didáctica de la E.F. Un enfoque constructivista. Barcelona: INDE.
- Devís Devís, J. (2002). La Educación Física, el Deporte y la Salud en el siglo XXI. Barcelona: INDE.
- Devís, J. y Peiró, C. (1997). Nuevas perspectivas curriculares en E.F.: la salud y los juegos modificados. Barcelona: Inde.
- Ferrer, F. y Montañana, R. (2015). Guía Básica de Formación "Primeros pasos para la integración curricular de las competencias clave en los centros educativos". Albacete
- Ferrer, F. y Montañana, R. (2016). Manual básico de evaluación 2016-17. Albacete.
- Guillén, R. (2000). Actividades en la naturaleza. Barcelona: INDE.

- Hernández Moreno, J. (2005). Análisis de las estructuras del juego deportivo. Barcelona: INDE.
- Junta de Comunidades de Castilla-La Mancha (2013). Decreto 66/2013, por el que se regula la respuesta a la diversidad del alumnado en la Comunidad Autónoma de Castilla-La Mancha. Toledo
- Junta de Comunidades de Castilla-La Mancha (2014). Decreto 54/2014, por el que se establece el currículo de la Educación Primaria en la Comunidad Autónoma de Castilla-La Mancha. Toledo
- Junta de Comunidades de Castilla-La Mancha (2014). Orden 5/08/2014, por la que se regulan la organización y la evaluación en la Educación Primaria en la comunidad autónoma de Castilla-La Mancha. Toledo.
- Junta de Comunidades de Castilla-La Mancha (2015). Resolución 11/03/2015 por la que se concreta la categorización, la ponderación y la asociación con las competencias clave, por áreas de conocimiento y cursos, de los estándares de aprendizaje evaluables, publicados en el Decreto 54/2014. Toledo.
- Linares, D. (1989). Expresión corporal y desarrollo psicomotor. Málaga: Ed. Unisport. Málaga
- Ministerio de Educación y Ciencia (2006). Ley Orgánica 2/2006, de 3 de mayo, de Educación (LOE). Madrid
- Ministerio de Educación y Ciencia (2006). Real Decreto 1513/2006, de 7 de diciembre, por el que se establecen las enseñanzas mínimas de la Educación primaria. Madrid.
- Ministerio de Educación y Ciencia (2013). Ley Orgánica 8/2013, de 9 de diciembre para la mejora de la calidad educativa (LOMCE). Madrid.
- Ministerio de Educación y Ciencia (2014). Real Decreto 126/2014, por el que se establece el currículo básico de la Educación Primaria. Madrid
- Ministerio de Educación y Ciencia (2015). Orden ECD/65/2015, de 21 de enero, por la que se describen las relaciones entre las competencias, los contenidos y los criterios de evaluación de la educación primaria, la educación secundaria obligatoria y el bachillerato. Madrid.
- Moreno Palos, C. (1992). Aspectos recreativos de los juegos y deportes tradicionales en España. Madrid: Gymnos.
- Motos Teruel, T. (1983). Iniciación a la expresión corporal. Barcelona: Ed. Humanitas
- Ortega Murcia, J. (2006). Cero al maltrato entre iguales.
- Peiró, C. (2003). Actividad motriz y Salud en la escuela. Barcelona: INDE.
- Pinos Quilez, M., 1997: Actividades y juegos de E.F. en la naturaleza. Madrid: Gymnos.
- Sánchez Bañuelos, F. (1992). Didáctica de la EF y el deporte. Madrid: Gymnos.

www.ingramcontent.com/pod-product-compliance
Lightning Source LLC
Chambersburg PA
CBHW081236090426
42738CB00016B/3329

* 9 7 8 8 4 9 9 9 3 9 5 8 2 *

What Lies Beyond the Frame

poems from the
Bridgewater International Poetry Festival 2017

Stan Galloway, editor
Elizabeth Liebl, associate editor

ENGLEWOOD, NJ

ISBN 978-1-936373-58-1

Published in the United States by Unbound Content, LLC, Englewood, NJ.
Cover art: © 2018 Katherine Hanna
Cover design and page layout: Steven Walker, Walker Creative Inc.

The poems in this collection are all original and previously unpublished with the exception of those listed in the credits page at the end of the volume.

SCRATCHING AGAINST THE FABRIC
Volume I, 2015

THEIR OWN BARE HANDS
Volume II, 2017

Preface

This anthology is the result of the Bridgewater International Poetry Festival. In 2017, the festival occurred in January and was held at Bridgewater College, a small school nestled in the Shenandoah Valley. The festival, as it grows, requires a fair amount of effort to host. To this end, the students of the January-based "interterm" class Writing Contemporary Poetry are enlisted to help with the festival. This is a lot of work for the students (of which I am one), but it is also an amazing opportunity, and I feel comfortable saying the festival wouldn't be the same without the dedicated work of those students.

In this anthology, we have used poems read at this year's festival to attempt to answer the question unasked by the title: what, exactly, lies beyond the frame? I hope that you find the answer here satisfactory enough to look further beyond your own frame, whether it be the frame of your laptop, your window, or your doorway. Enjoy.

Elizabeth Liebl
Associate Editor

The title of this anthology is taken from Susan Notar's "Hands with Grapes," an ekphrastic poem based on an Alfred Steiglitz photograph of Georgia O'Keefe. The literal picture has borders, a traditional frame whether material or the absence of continuance. "What lies beyond the frame" names the un-namable and challenges our human attempts to categorize our life experiences, to keep things framed. For every literal experience there is the ineffable doppelgänger, always the tugging suggestion that there is more to what we sense than we can quantify. The poet, in similar ways, frames images and experiences, all the while conscious of the fact that much more lies outside the frame than inside. What the poet captures may be that traditional sepia moment or conversely its impatience with its own conventions. In the end, every attempt to capture what lies beyond the frame fails because it establishes a new frame, like trying to look at darkness with a flashlight; but we are not the poorer for that. Every moment chronicled in a poem (or music or art or theatre) adds one more facet to the carving of human identity.

With this anthology, our third, we mark a move from our biennial pattern to an annual production. We also will move from January to May. That in itself is symbolic of our growth, maturing from winter into spring. Condensing the work of the festival into these new parameters means that we are always working on the next event. But life is that way for all of us. If you cannot attend the festival that we host each year, with this anthology and those that came before and will follow, you can sample what lies beyond the frame.

Thank you for picking up this volume. Proceeds from the festival anthologies are used to assist international poets in attending the festival. Donations also can be made at the festival's web site.

Stan Galloway
Editor

Contents

WHAT LIES BEYOND THE FRAME: ON POETRY AS IMPOSSIBLE TRANSLATION

Introduction by Seth Michelson

In homage to the celebrated Modernist poet Hart Crane, who committed suicide in 1932 at age thirty-two by leaping from a New York-bound steamship into the Gulf of Mexico, the contemporary U.S. poet Stan Galloway opens his poem "To Sleep" by intimating that

[o]n nights when I lie achingly alone,
I understand the man
whose poetry was not enough
to cauterize the cuts of disaffection.

And it is precisely Galloway's articulation of disaffection that I aim to discuss herein. Most immediately, it offers a clarifying trope for framing this international anthology of poetry exploring "what lies beyond the frame." More broadly, through the logic of that tropology, it introduces the grounds for theorizing the very limits of poetic possibility itself.

In short, disaffection in "To Sleep" is the provocation of poetry, which importantly always already fails it. That is, disaffection is the furious upsurge of psychic and cognitive tumult that compels the writer to the page, where she wrongly presumes her ascription of poetic language to that tumult to be somehow capable of becalming it. Yet it doesn't. Disaffection lies beyond the frame of poetry. Or as Galloway explains it, poetry is not enough.

Moreover, if disaffection both provokes and exceeds poetry, then this is also to say that the grounds for poetry are always already everywhere. Disaffection circumscribes and courses through the poet, with its maelstrom of emotion inundating her consciousness and by extension suffusing her process of writing poetry. And when in that process she discovers yet again that poetry is not enough—when poetry reveals itself inevitably to be inadequate to the task of reckoning and rendering disaffection to the relief of the poet—she is struck by the agonistic insight that the only possible relief to the irreconcilable struggle is "to sleep."

Until the arrival of sleep, she must battle like Galloway and Crane in the thralls of a life of poetry-making and its inevitable aftermath of despair in the wake of each poem's failure. In other words, in his poem about the inadequacy of poetry to redress disaffection, Galloway is offering us an interesting ars poetica, or rather an anti-ars poetica, an anti-poetry. He is arguing for a crucial recognition of poetry's incapacity. He hopes to elucidate for his readers that which escapes poetic capture, what lies beyond its frame, where poetry is not enough.

In this manner, the ars poetica might bring to mind the oeuvre of the great Chilean poet Nicanor Parra (b. 1914), who founded anti-poesía, or anti-poetry in the Americas. Unlike Crane's masterful verbal dexterity and breathtaking experimental imagery, Parra builds his anti-poetry out of demotic, prosaic language, which he sets in direct juxtaposition with the high pathos of the poem to create its driving, ironic tension. This is exemplified by Parra's much anthologized ars poetica "Letters from a Poet in a Chair," wherein he writes, for example:

Young poets
Say whatever you want
Pick your own style
Too much blood has gone under the bridge
To still believe—I believe—
That there's only one way to cross the road:
You can do anything in poetry.

Here one reads the tension born of the clash of simple diction with intense feeling in the juxtaposition of a plainspoken, allusive sketch of poetic historiography with an exhortation to poets to persist in their serious poetic play. More immediately, you are soon to sample a marvelous diversity of poets who have been able to "pick [their] own style" and follow it to create seemingly limitless "way[s] to cross the road." Nevertheless, as Galloway argues, "poetry [is] not enough." Disaffection persists. The poet's despair remains. And importantly, too, Parra addresses that intrinsic failure.

For Parra the inadequacy of poetry is foundational. For example, in the aforementioned poem, he goes on to suggest that "[t]he poet's job is / [t]o improve on the blank page / [and] I don't think that's possible." In other words, like Galloway, Parra is intimating to the reader that poetry is not enough. Poetry fails. At its best, it can merely allude to what lies beyond its frame.

Interestingly, too, Crane also reveals this devastating truth, albeit through his distinct style. For example, in the second stanza of his masterpiece "To Brooklyn Bridge," he writes:

Then, with inviolate curve, forsake our eyes
As apparitional as sails that cross

Some page of figures to be filed away;
—Till elevators drop us from our day . . .

Here, the language is clearly more elevated than Parra's, and the use of rhythm and form more intricate, but the verse nevertheless shares in the timbre of both Parra's and Galloway's despair. In Crane's case, it emerges from both the images of ephemerality and the images of one's loss of agency in relation to the industrialized landscape, however stunningly magnificent and seemingly propitious certain technologies like sweeping bridges and high elevators.

Furthermore, Crane's poem, like Galloway's, and like the collected verse in this anthology, exemplifies Parra's claim that "[y]ou can do anything in poetry." Nevertheless, as Parra explains, no matter how she tries, the poet's job is predetermined to fail; her poetic striving is impossible. She will "pick [her] own style," attempt "to cross the road," and ultimately be forced to concede that poetry is not enough; disaffection exceeds it and remains.

Worse, as Galloway confides, the poet is thereupon left to suffer the "cuts of disaffection," which are intensified by her plangent recognition of the inadequacy of her art. Thus she is remanded to an aching loneliness born of the excess or ineradicable remainder of disaffection, and her helplessness as poet.

For Galloway, that enduring double despair is his psychic link to Crane. It is also the implied impetus of Crane's suicide. It is why, as Galloway writes, Crane chose "open water off a steamship's stern / (as good as any bridge or urban cement ledge) / to one more day of struggle." And on achingly lonely nights, Galloway, too, feels this deeply. In fact it drives him to intimate to his readers that in such moments of despair, "[w]hat I crave is / to be engulfed by something, / whether water or a simple sleep."

Of note, this might also prompt one to ask what of disaffection can a poem render? What, if anything, can poetry do in the face of disaffection? And perhaps in response, one might turn again to the poem "To Sleep" for helpful insights. For example, the poem pivots on a crucial paradox: It is a poem about poetry's inability to represent disaffection, yet it re-presents this to the reader via poem that quite affectively communicates the pathos of the poet's disaffection.

Accordingly one might argue that the presentation of disaffection in "To Sleep" is paradoxically made present by its absence. In other words, the poem is allusive, indicating that which escapes it by tracing its outline like a negative space drawing, whereby the poem is mere background, mere secondary detail to foreground and frame the ineluctable. Hence

Galloway's poem, like Crane's, summons and outlines disaffection, however much its direct and unmediated experience escapes the poem.

Interestingly, too, in this manner, Galloway's enunciation of the despair of the poet in reckoning poetry's inability to render disaffection is a paradoxically successful rendering of the failures of the poet to translate disaffection into verse. Via that logic, one could extrapolate further that "To Sleep" is in fact an ars poetica defining poetry as translation. More properly, it is an ars poetica defining poetry as failed translation, or of poetry as an exploration of the intrinsic inadequacies, inabilities, and failures of translation, which can cause despair. Unable to cauterize disaffection's cuts by writing, the poet bleeds out; she goes to sleep.

This is also to say that disaffection cannot be translated into poetry, except in the negative space hewn by failed attempts at its indirect rendering. In other words, to write a poetry of disaffection is to try but fail to translate its untranslatability for the reader. It is to strive impossibly to transfer to her the experience of suffering poetry's inability to render disaffection for the reader and to neutralize it for the writer. Hence Galloway's anti-poetry, whereby poetry is a reckoning of the untranslatable. The poetic process is not enough. Translational processes like poetry always already fail.

Of note, such claims are by no means new to literary studies. Rather, to build upon Parra's figure, Galloway's examination of "what lies beyond the frame" is but one more "way to cross the road" of life. And one might trace such critical frameworks back in time to the Platonic criticism of poetry as mere imitation, for example, which is to say poetry fails as a merely reductive form of mimesis of ideas.

Nevertheless, as Parra and many others have insisted, one must not forget the power of play in such intrinsically failed poetic processes. Such play is as evident in Parra's anti-poetic tone as in Crane's Modernist diction. Likewise it courses through "To Sleep," even as Galloway's aching loneliness overwhelms him.

That defiant belief in the importance of play, however friable, however willfully naïve, permeates the verse in this anthology of poetry impossibly striving to reckon that which lies beyond the frame. As such, this book might even cohere into a literary mosaic of poetries of disaffection. In that sense, each poem herein is an individuated, spectral testimony to each poet's impossible play, whereby she has struggled in her own style to render in language the untranslatable.

To illustrate this insistence on the necessity of translational poetic play in the face of the genre's intrinsic failure, one might look again to "To Sleep," where Galloway's admission of poetry's inadequacy is nevertheless crafted with vibrant, vital, and delicate poetic care. Moreover, Galloway's tragic pleasure in poetic play in the face of disaffection is clarified and amplified by juxtaposing "To Sleep" with three translations of it for the 2017 Bridgewater International Poetry Festival.

More specifically, for the festival, "To Sleep" was translated into Arabic by Nadia Boudidah as "إلى الرّقاد," into German by Geraldine Poppke Suter as "Dem Schlaf," and into Spanish by Mahan Ellison as "A Dormir," and the playful, impossible process of each translator's poetic translation is revealing in itself and in relation to the other poems in the cluster. That is, all four iterations of the poem quite notably offer a postponement through poetic play of Galloway's achievement of his moribund desire for a:

Morphean release
with Lethe's drug
that I might be reborn
forgetful of the fight

In other words, the impulse to sleep is deferred by the very writing that is inadequate to address it. Hence the poem might be inadequate to disaffection, but the poem through its poetic play nevertheless contests the death drive. Poetry enacts a life in the face of its imminent, impending demise. Poetry is thereby an action against dying. It is an act of existing, even in a poem about the death drive's omnipresent, ineluctable, and voracious omnipotence.

Perhaps the poem "To Sleep," then, and the poem in relation to its trifold translation, is also to be understood as a counterintuitive but affirming assertion of vitality through its poetic enunciation of suicidal impulses. That is, "To Sleep," and its ramifying extensions into translations, enacts a multifaceted genesis through and against dying. It is a celebration of growth, transformation, and endurance via a marking of death's inevitability. For however contrary to the surface of the narrative content of all four poems, they each showcase the eruption of the struggle to translate disaffection into verse and the consequent postponement of death by the process of poetry writing.

In other words, the intrinsic failure of verse is mobilized within and across languages here, with each poem affirming life through play even while ruminating on the inexorability of a decline to death. Moreover, by intertwining itself in multiple translations, and by imbricating itself in multiple translators' lives, the death drive is redirected into a poetic activity of creation; these four poets, for example, interlace themselves through poetry-making into a compounding poetic network of clarifying, if allusive, articulations of the impending disarticulation of self. And in this manner, such struggle with death is life-sustaining, and perhaps even life-making.

And this might finally be the most important claim herein to the potentiality of poetry: every poem, however flawed and inadequate, and in whatever style the poet might pick, pays homage to the ephemeral yet fierce force of poetry to forge new ways of being in, of, and against death. Poetry creates connections that foster life. Poetry binds and nourishes. It creates new solidarities and affinities against dying by acknowledging the inevitability of decay in life even as it asserts its regeneration.

By extension, one of the great strengths of poetry is its capacity to generate sociality, even if one must always already concede the inability of sociality to save an individuated life. For whether alone or in collectives, we as living beings will never know in itself that which lies beyond the frame, yet concomitantly poetry offers each individuated poet and reader the possibility to join and conjoin through verse in an effort to strive impossibly towards knowing and understanding it.

Furthermore, there is consolation in such activity, even when agonistically treading the liminal thresholds of life's outermost reaches. This is also to say that even when confronting the despair of an epiphanic realization like Galloway's that poetry is not enough, one discovers the solace of companionship in struggle; one finds friendship in the dark; Galloway finds Crane; we find Parra and them; you find this anthology; translators find poets. And yet despite it all, this is not enough. Disaffection endures. Death exceeds poetry.

Nevertheless, with and against disaffection and death, poetic potentiality persists, too. Each poetic experience offers itself as an active eruption into being. It is the evental activity of becoming. Each poetic action is a light, a star coming into being, augmenting the vast and pulsating network of lights in even the loneliest night sky.

And it is precisely in spite and because of its inherent inadequacy that poetry can cultivate the conditions for such deep, intense, and enriching engagements of inter- and intrapersonal vitality. My hope, dear reader, is for you to savor it in the pages to come.

To Sleep

Stan Galloway

On nights when I lie achingly alone,
I understand the man
whose poetry was not enough
to cauterize the cuts of disaffection,
choosing open water off a steamship's stern
(as good as any bridge or urban cement ledge)
to one more day of struggle.

To be engulfed by something,
whether water or a simple sleep,
is what I crave,
but both of us are one key short
of that obscure approval
that, by the name we give it,
leaves us barricaded in an empty street.

Come, Morphean release
with Lethe's drug
that I might be reborn
forgetful of the fight
so I will have the strength to take it on again
the way that Helios initiates the chariot
as if it were the first time horses ever flew.

A Dormir

Stan Galloway
Spanish Translation by Mahan Ellison

En las noches cuando me acuesto dolorosamente solo,
entiendo al hombre
cuya poesía no podía
cauterizar las incisiones de la desafección,
el que escogió el agua abierta de la popa de un barco de vapor
(tan buena como cualquier puente o cornisa urbana de cemento)
a un día más de luchar.

Ser tragado por algo,
sea agua o un sueño sencillo,
es lo que anhelo,
pero a nosotros nos falta algo clave
de esta aprobación oscura
que, por el nombre que lo damos,
nos deja atrapados en una calle vacía.

Ven, liberación morfea
con la droga de Lete
para que yo me renazca
desmemoriado de la lucha
para que tenga la fuerza para tomarla de nuevo
como inicia Helio la cuadriga
como si fuera la primera vez que volaran los caballos.

Dem Schlaf

Stan Galloway
German Translation by Geraldine Suter

In Nächten, in denen ich schmerzend allein da liege,
verstehe ich den Mann,
dessen Gedichte nicht genug waren,
um die Wunden der Unzufriedenheit wegzuätzen,
das offene Wasser am Heck eines Dampfboots wählend
(ebenso gut wie jede Brücke oder städtische Betonkante)
anstatt noch einen Tag des Kampfes.

Von etwas umschlossen zu sein,
sei es Wasser oder einfach Schlaf,
das ist es wonach ich mich sehne,
doch fehlt uns beiden je ein Ton
dieser schleierhaften Anerkennung
die uns, mit dem Namen, den wir ihr geben,
verbarrikadiert auf einer leeren Straße zurück lässt.

Komm, Morpheus' Erlösung
mit Lethes Droge
dass ich wiedergeboren sein mag
den Kampf vergessend,
damit ich die Kraft habe ihn wieder aufzunehmen
so wie Helios den (Streit)wagen in Gang setzt,
als ob es das erste Mal wäre, dass Pferde flögen.

إلـى الرّقـاد

Stan Galloway
Arabic Translation by Nadia Boudidah

إلـى الرّقـاد

لهارت كراين

في تلك اللّيالي عندما أختلي في وحدة موجعة
أفهم كنه ذلك الرّجل الّذي
لم يكن بوسع شعره
كيّ جراح الجفاء وتضميدها
مؤثرا الإرتماء في عرض البحر من
ذنب متن باخرة
(مثلها مثل أيّ جسر أو حافّة اسمنتيّة)
على تحمّل يوم آخر من النّضال

فأنا أتوق إلى أن يغمرني شيء ما
سواء أكان الماء أم سنة من النّوم
بيد أنّ كلينا قاربنا على الخضوع لذلك الوفاق الغائم
الذّي، بما منحناه من اسم،
يتركنا مأسورين في شارع مقفر قاتم

فليأتوني بتعويذة تخدّر احساسي
وعقار إلاه النّسيان
عسى أن أبعث من سباتي
غافلا عن كلّ تلك الصّراعات
حتّى أقوى على مجابهتها بثبات
تماما كما تولّى هيليوس زمام العربة
كما لو كانت الخيول تحلّق لأوّل مرّة أبدا

The Black North Road

George Perreault

In this steady welcome rain a billboard calls out
today's the Sabbath, Sunday, the mark of the Beast,
and we may have gone to school with children
of that faith, proud in election to such narrow company,
or not—who's to say how these histories will run.

Next door to our grade school was a church, mainline
no doubt, but not my family's, though the winsome girls
descended from heretics proved ever gentle-mouthed
and breathless to embrace those half-forgotten hayrides
under harvest moons—that's all I can remember.

In our pidgin, many moons ago great Papisse Conewa,
Child of the Bear, would camp at Pawtucket Falls,
a mighty shaman raising thunderstorms at will, our town
just deer tracks in a wilderness north of the Merrimack,
a frontier of brooks and bogs, rich in fish and timber.

Then farmers cleared trees for pastures, naming these
curving roads for where they led—Loon Hill and Marsh
Hill, Old Meadow Road, Long Pond and Lakeview—
or what was built there—Bridge Street, School or Mill,
Prides Crossing—a layered irony too rich to forget.

Our lessons the usual gloss from Pilgrims to King Phillip
to Valley Forge, manifest destinies and the uncivil carnage
through which we have assumed our greatness, cowboys
and Indians, sea to shining sea, and on bright yellow buses
cruising The Black North Road we never asked why—

so we never learned that name was not merely direction but
stubborn fact—emancipated slaves were here from the start
hacking a life from the stony soil, while their Railroad
was covered wagons late at night, fugitives heading up
to New Hampshire huddled under straw and vegetables,

for there were laws after all, and while some men stood
righteous, others would dutifully bind over brothers and
sisters to the iron rule of commerce, ship people back like
commodities when intermingled, North and South alike,
enslaved Negroes and Natives served our greed.

So The Black North was people first—Hart and Hartwell,
Lew and Freeman—they had papers, permission to be
human while through this land slid more, underground,
though elders claimed it was never us but always others
whose hands caressed the whip at home and abroad.

It was Nazis, Gypsies and Jews, Turks and Armenians,
or African tribes no one can ever keep straight, pink
triangles or godless Reds—we learned there's always
someone to hate, and today can be a true Sabbath if only
The Black North Road stays unshackled in our hearts.

Boy Howdy

Hiram Larew

Modern life hurts me—
Would that I could die in the arms
Of seed catalogues
Or turn over in a bed and feel
Snow coming in the window

My father taught me to wave at life from
Cherished corners
His coat pockets were really my teenage years

Carry on is how I feel now—

So may these lines become as strikingly handsome
As hands on shoulders
May they cause strangers to look up again and again
May the hope in these lines age well like chewed pencils
Or turn into stale crumbs
That birds will fight over.

A Breach of Etiquette

Annmarie Lockhart

I called someone an asshole today.
On Facebook. Dick, a
"friend" of a "friend."

After which he said I must be angry.
As if there is something shameful
about being angry.

I didn't comment further,
didn't say:
Yes, Dick, I am angry.
I am fucking furious because
I see another dead black
boy and no justice.

I didn't say:
Twice in my life I've been pregnant
and cried with relief when I learned
that all three of my biracial children
would be girls. I cried, Dick,
because I had been afraid
I'd end up burying three black sons.
And yes, you're right, Dick. That makes
me angry. That should make me
and pretty much everyone angry.

I didn't say:
Just another dead black boy, whose life
is worth less today than when he would
only have counted as three-fifths of a man
some 200 years back. That is some
ass-backwards progress, Dick.

I didn't say:
So I guess we're both right, Dick: I am angry.
And you are an asshole.

Convergence

Caroline Brae

Intrigued by my voiceless image
A face barely seen beneath
Sunglasses, lime green floppy hat,
And plaid wool scarf
A temporary glimpse
Of the woman behind the lens
Or hidden in the shadowy reflections
Of a chapel window honoring
Fallen soldiers from an uncivil war
It isn't a game we play
It is an exchange in an electronic world
Where photos are shared in instant squares
With captions sometimes short
Other times long, with the resulting
Longing of places and people
Ones you can sense, but cannot touch
Nights are long and
Mornings come early
Conversing with a friend
Across invisible lines
When there are no words
Or explanations for feelings
For those unseen, illuminating
Beings of light whose frames
Create a sense of connection
In the silence of midair

Fucked

Marc Harshman

He is deaf from the whining scream of the chainsaw, and is sweating under a thinning, November sun. There must have been some way to avoid this hellhole in the Middle East. When he had seen the pictures on the screen last night, something had knotted in his belly. But here, at least, this morning, the work felt good, the bright, interior heart of the tree exposed like this. Fuck politics. There were wormholes. Some people liked them in their furniture. Antique. He was fifty-nine years old. And lately it felt old. *Antique*. Christ, what he wouldn't give for a beer and a chance to get laid by that girl at Tommy's. She was a bright thing. He'd vote the bastards out of office if any other bastards would do any better. The white house down below had rung the cops once about his chain-sawing on Sunday. Fuck the neighbors and their Sunday. Fuck the neighbors and their lament about the old elm. Fuck everyone. What was it his son had said in that poem. "*Fuck* was a strong word, an Anglo Saxon word, a good word that gets the job done." He was sharp, that boy of his, despite his politics. Funny how the kid could be so sharp and dumb all at once. How anyone could believe in those sissy liberal assholes, but worse, he began to think, how could anyone believe anything at all? Maybe all he needed was to introduce his son to Sheila down there at Tommy's. Maybe that was all anyone ever really needed. It was worth a try. One more cut and he'd have the hour in and enough firewood for a month. It felt good. But, Jesus, those little kids. That was what bugged him. Little kids, parts of their bodies just strewn across the ground like windblown trash. And our boys did this? Something was fucked . . . big time.

The Cleveland Indians Hosting the Chicago Cubs in the First Game of the 2016 World Series, or Thoughts Before They Poke a Hole in My Chest

Barry Gross

Does THE-END have a gender pronoun?
If IT should brush a fingered breath across my shaved chest
I hope it resists temptation to take,
and moves along
and mutters in distraction:
"I'll be this way again.
Another day, another day,
I'll see him another day."

A Young Man of Our Times

Albert Russo

He's young, tall and slim,
muscled, just enough not to look
like those pin-up guys

he's bright and speedy
doesn't like to repeat
what he's told me twice

he's as handsome as
a movie star, but doesn't make
a fuss about his looks

he's been spotted
by a film agent
and models at times

he's also acted
in a TV series
but never informed me

'keep mum about it'
he says to me once I knew
'no publicity'

He's always dreamt
of becoming an actor
but works in fashion

his managers like him
and so does most of his team
he's kind and efficient

so much so that
some find him too reserved
while others too serious

people don't always know
how to evaluate him
which is disturbing

he's so honest
they take advantage of him
and he feels uneasy

that young man is now
married to a lovely girl
they have a blue-eyed cat
he's the son I adore

Terror Is the Placebo

Written after Reading George Orwell's *1984* in Julia's Voice

Mattie Quesenberry Smith

Terror is a placebo for what you might have been.
The wyrm eats the difference, so you swallow Victory Gin.
We will grab the rest when we can: proper white bread,
A little jar of jam, coffee, sugar in brown paper packets,
A little bit of tea. We have stolen
Inner Party treats, swallow what we can,
Pleasing *no one* but your flesh. Turn me around.
My face is made, and I bought a woman's frock.

Forget the clock, bell towers, oranges, and the lemons.
Don't mention you have forgotten the bells of St. Clements:
My face is made and I have brought a white frock—
Pull up your trousers and straighten the sash—
That scarlet gash, manhandled in Party sunsets.
Swallow, pleasing no one but your flesh;
Turn me around now; my face is made;
I brought a frock that is Woman's.

Forget the clock towers, the oranges, and the lemons;
Swallow up the terror, lap it like a dog; it's placebo from the rest.
We please no one but your flesh, so pull up your trousers,
Forget the rest, the bell-clock and the horrors, as you pull up
Your trousers and grab my sash—clock hands crack black—
Let the whole thing fall. It is time, after all,
For them to take the tea and leave the terror,
Bidden to drop a snatch around our waists.

We are shaken, shaken, shaken for forgetfulness from disease:
The bells, they are a singing, and light pours from the East,
But we, we are remembering terror from the towers:
Clocks wind without arrest. It is you: yes, somehow
You have forgotten to bring the chopper for the light;
Somewhere you have forgotten the dead man's rite;

Something is the mnemonic device, if only this remembrance:
you forgot.
Someday, this day, you cannot help but remember: *Placebo Domino.*
Instead, you take the terror and placebo for the rest.

Wondering Why While Wandering Where

Andrew Manyika

Time spent walking the earth wears down the sole

Dust
Whilst packing the last of our prized possessions,
Moving things we thought we'd planted,
And letting emptiness reprise it's position,
We turn our home into a mere house
and I come across an old pair of shoes
They are well-worn and from the process of so becoming,
are worn down. Scuffed at the front, warm to the feel,
And torn at the heel
I try to remember them being new,
And all the places they've been since then
It amuses me to think that shoes, having tongues but no eyes,
cannot tell of all the places they've seen
So, these shoes, that have moved me through every plausible place,
I now remove to put them away
In so doing, I catch sight of the heel and it's curvature strikes me,
I am wondering where the rubber that had been this sole has gone
In leaving it's imprint on the earth,
Did it also leave little pieces of itself behind,
Like calling cards for the ground?
And all that displaced dust?
Did it creep into the grooves of the sole so that,
Knowingly or not, I brought little pieces of everywhere,
Here, to our home.
Which, once these shoes are packed, will become only a house?
In them I've walked so many miles, so many miles . . .
Time spent walking the earth wears down the soul

Home
We've packed everything that needed packing,
And stacked every box that needed stacking,
And as strangers gut my home,

I say as little as possible because every sound now carries an echo
And every echo makes it harder to let go and realise,

This is no longer my place,
As silence takes hold of every audible space
I stand looking at the thin film of dust on all the surfaces,
You grab my arm and we remark together how it settled so easily on our dreams
Like little pieces of everywhere stifling little pieces of us
Dreams die slow deaths and there is nothing gentle about their passing,
All it takes for a pen to bleed is, in the right place,
A touch and a little pressure,
As tears blur my vision, I think perhaps my soul is much like a pen
You grab my arm again and tell me,
"It's time"
You are not wrong,
We have filled the quota of memories to be made here
And it's a long way to the new house,
Between here and there are so many miles, so many miles....

To Sir Bob, With Love

Annmarie Lockhart

This poem is not about love

but taking in that mix: one part
Dylan, two parts Van Morrison, a pinch
of Jagger and a dash of Lord Byron

is heady stuff.

He said "I'm responsible for two of the worst
songs in history." And he has a point.
After all, he built punk progressions
on Irish melodies. He stayed up all night, firing off love
like rockets, prophesying psychopathic Mondays.

But 1984 was a simpler time. One phone call
to Midge Ure and three weeks later, a song was
written. One marathon recording session
later, the brightest lights of British pop were
throwing their arms around the world at
Christmastime.

Yes, those were simpler times.

In these times, the editor in me fights
the urge to change "the bitter sting of tears"
to "the bitter stream of tears." The socially
aware mom in me acknowledges the
blithe imperialism of wondering whether
a multitude possesses consciousness
of a calendar.

Still, those were simpler times.

And it was easy to believe that a song
could change the world. Hearts and hands
were open and hope felt like more than an empty
word in a candidate's slogan. For a few brief
moments, the well-fed and the hungry shared

the same table.

It was a simpler time. Simple enough for Dublin's kinetic madman to flip off the world and feed it in one smooth gesture.

Eternal June

Annmarie Lockhart

This poem is not about hate.

I remember how it feels to be
hungry, waiting in sunrise tatters
to be reclaimed
to feel exceptional
waiting on Sunday
for Monday's broken promise
for the run of a lifetime
scavenged from scraps
of yesterday.

The pervasiveness
of possibility means
I might be a sheep
in wolf's clothing
stealing plot, character,
and, always, hope
lifting last lines from
my sifted poems

or I could just as easily be
five liquid drops of mercury
ladybugs clustered red, black,
yellow
a grainy picture
of ingrained freedoms
and non white flight.

This poem is about hope.

Tiger Lilies

Mark Fitzgerald

As if to charm unkempt borders,
broken fences and weathered walls,
as if to grace a country road—they bloom
in fire, in spotted trumpets that call

upon a summer day. What orange
dream lives on like a bottomless thirst
in the lilies I saw from a distance
at the edge of the woods as a child?

I can't recall whether they spoke
to me then as a stay against discontent
or later in a watercolor of a cherished
time. Whether they cured me of sorrow

as I came closer, I can't say.
But something born from innocence
awoke in the petals which together made
a face that seemed to know me

as much as summer and all
of its changes. I dreamt that face
was a friend who helped me learn
the many ways of healing, of never

giving up, of giving over
to butterflies that rise without sound
above the stamens, as if in their wings
they held the light of angels.

Carousel Man

Steven Knepper

Nobody trusts a carnie. That's a fact.
Some moms don't even let me lift their kid
Up on a horse for fear I have designs.
When a local church meets at the grounds
I feel the eyes when I get passed the plate.
I have a trailer in the Poconos
And work the ski resorts all winter long,
Make furniture and cabinets on the side
To customize those overpriced chalets.
This job ain't one I need to make ends meet.

Not that the carnie crew is full of saints.
I'm careful where I put my wallet down.
But bosses try to weed the perverts out
Because they know that spot won't wash away—
They'd lose their contracts when it hit the papers.

I've seen some awful things at carnivals,
But carnies weren't involved in most of them.
One place was running dog fights after hours.
I couldn't sleep for all the yelps and growls.
One time I saw a woman whip her kid
With plastic pipe out in the parking lot.
I served an army stint right out of school
But never saw a killing till this job—
Some boy that won a switchblade tossing rings
And got the itch to try it right away.
Meth has made things worse in recent years,
With tweekers turning tricks in port-a-johns
Or raiding rides at night for parts and wire,
Their caved-in mugs as pale as graveyard ghouls.

I'm giving you the wrong impression, though.
The apple core ain't close to rotten yet.
There's still a magic in the carnival—
The laughter that you hear, the way the light
Looks on the spinning Ferris wheel at night,
How it glistens on the children's eyes

When they go round and round the carousel.
The parents wear this smile that's bittersweet
Because they want to give their kid a life
Just like a pony ride that never ends.

The carousel's a marvelous machine.
I don't know where the company got this one.
It's really something else—our finest ride.
I'd sooner quit than work the giant slide
Or pirate ship with all those snotty teens.
It has an inner row that rises up
And down, an outer row that's fixed for tots—
Bucking broncos, regal quarter horses,
Prancing unicorns with golden horns,
Even saddled ostriches and seals
If you prefer to ride a wilder mount.

Two years ago I made a horse for it.
A new guy didn't look before he backed
Into the setup zone and mangled one.
It bothered me to see that empty pole.
I spent my free time carving linden wood
That winter. Didn't take the extra jobs.
I ordered books off of the Internet,
And even visited a shop in Jersey.
I worked by hand, with chisels and a mallet.
My first one was a costly, clunky dud
But then I got the hang of it and carved
The kind of steed to make a cowboy proud,
An appaloosa with its chestnut spots,
Varnish adding shine to every curve.

I took him in my truck that spring when I
Reported to the buildings where the company
Winterizes rides and does repairs.
Turns out they'd already ordered one.
Mine never left my truck bed till the fall.
I won't deny that stung. I'd often thought
About the kids who'd race to get him first,
About the light that'd catch him as he turned.
He sat in my garage for half a year,

Collecting dust and bird shit in a corner.
But this past spring I showed him to the lady
Who manages our little trailer park.
She plants some flowers by the northern gate.
I made a post and mounted him out there
So that he's leaping over hyacinths.
It's not exactly what I had in mind,
But he'll still stir some wonder in the world.

Brown Rabbit

John Berry

The brown rabbit I drew
I remember because it looked like a rabbit.

And I can say with a high degree of authority
it was indeed brown as that is what was written
on the crayon I used, and crayons do not lie.

It was a study in profile, and had you been touring
Mrs. Jennings 2nd grade classroom in 1973, and happened
to be facing North when you saw it, the rabbit
would have been turned to the East
where the Sun had broken
its ancient moorings.

You also would have noticed the remarkable precision
in the shape of the rabbit; proportioned well, head neither
too large or small for its body, ears outlined in a passable
representation of three dimensions—
one disappearing behind the other, both angling
up and back from the nibbling creatures head.

Now, because he was pictured crouched on the ground
in the classical posture of rabbit at rest,
you would only have seen his two right legs;
the curve of the powerful haunch like a warrior's shield
against his belly, speedy paw outstretched like
a lance to his heart, his gentle foreleg (the one I believe
is taken for lucky) resting under his shoulder.

The pink nose, now, was perfect. A simple triangular shape,
easy to color, and though the eyes are said to be one of
the artist's most difficult challenges, being the windows,
they are, to the soul, I settled for a circle and the crayon
labeled 'black'. I felt it more important to place it well
than to agonize over that, which in nature, is still
a circle of black.

It should be noted that the grasses where he posed
were no mere stabs of green, but little tufts, gently tapered,
as the blades they are. Some even overlaying his soft
brown fur, again, to establish the feeling of a third
dimension.

As anyone familiar with crayons will tell you,
the heavier the hand, the bolder the color, and so it was
only with the lightest touch of powder blue that I sketched
the sky, leaving out any cloudy embellishments, no
lemon-yellow sun in the frame.

And last I remember the cotton-tail—
and the fear I held in my hand when reaching for that
pure white crayon. It was as if the entire portrait
hinged on the success or failure of this detail.
There could be no outline here, no basic black sketch
to fill in later with white. No, here was the crux. Here
was where I would trust or fail, holding the pure and
unblemished. Holding the innocence. For what would a
cotton-tail be without its cotton? At seven years of age
I doubt I pondered long this execution of innocence
before taking a breath
and beginning.

Yes, I remember the brown rabbit who faced East
as though he looked not to a new day of perfect orange
carrots, but to the recent past and a gallery of houses
made of sticks with curls of smoke rising from their leaning
chimneys, amorphous green blobs of color painting the trees.

And I remember the surprise and delight in Mrs. Jennings eyes.
I remember how proud I was to be featured on the sea-foam
wall where we, the ones who executed innocence
with precision, were held up as examples
to those, uncaring, as yet
if pure white crayons
bled into the other
colors.

The Color Wheel

George Perreault

Coming down the stone steps of St. Thomas, past
their sign advising *Watch your step*, wondering
if their concern's theological or just a legal shield—
the plaintiff was clearly cautioned your honor—

I overheard a middle-aged woman explaining
it's that color that's kinda between red and blue,
and I check myself, sotto voce—*purple… perhaps you mean the color*
purple—but then,

already drunk on stained glass, I'm sliding
toward forgiveness, which flares up fuchsia,
that plummy word with accents of burgundy and
bordeaux, taking a garden path among iris and lilac,

wisteria and violets, lavender, arbors thickened
with dusky handfuls of concord grapes, recalling
seascapes with indigo and periwinkle, a sky sliding
through magenta, amethyst and heather, moon rising

into clouds briefly marooned, and aren't we all
abandoned on some island abundant with sand, sepia
and chestnut, more greens than we could ever name,
those jewels sprawled between blue and yellow like

moldavite in the strewn fields, peridot, emerald and jade,
malachite, tsavorite, tourmaline and noble serpentine,
alexandrite prized for its color shifts, day or night,
and, yes, sapphire and garnet too, various as faces

passing on the sidewalk, voices filled with inflections,
text and subtext reflecting half-forgotten childhoods
and yesterday's history, colored by the grace of light
ever-changing somewhere between red and blue.

Grandmother at the Dressmakers'

for Bonnie Thurston

Marc Harshman

A bolt of heavy, cobalt gabardine,
shot with silver and scarlet threads,
lay across the cutting table.
It was July. The overhead fan threw slow shadows
upon the patterned, tin ceiling.
The neckline of Grandma's cotton housedress
had grown dark with sweat.
The street outside, Mulberry, was empty—it was that hot.
Grandma, however, made lists and did not move from them.
A few minutes, that's all.
I did not chafe too much at the familiar words
heard in grocery, at the neighbor's fence,
though always
my hand was tugging at her sleeve.
Bored, yes, but content enough, able
to wait for the promises: lemonade, ice cream, cookies.
It was to be an elbow's length longer than the yardstick.
There was tracing paper, thimbles, tweezers, bodkins,
and pinking shears with their intriguing teeth.
I took it all in, bothering and circling the women
with questions, anxious to know as much here
as I did in the barnyard with Father.
It was not poetry. Not yet. But it was life as I knew it
and I was keen to know it more, to keep gathering
as I did berries and stamps and pebbles,
to see what rarities might show up, sparkle and speak:
muscled cloth, scissor slash, and how precision
might be wedded to beauty,
to be the kind of gatherer
who would not starve
even if my clothes grow thin
and I can't find much to say for myself
other than I am still here,
tugging at her sleeve.

Good Girls

Dawn Leas

learn the difference
between second
and third bases
from older girls
while listening
to *Tapestry*
in the back bedroom
of a chilly duplex,
parents' hushed talk
floating up through
the floor vents.

Good girls write
Mrs. Houdak
with fancy curlicues
in the back
of their Mead binders,
marry first loves.

Good girls don't play
Spin the Bottle,
hearts racing
in the back
of a coat closet,
don't even think
about strip poker.

Good girls don't do
7 a.m. walks of shame,
or hang on front porches
with frat boys
drinking and smoking,
but go to Confession
on Saturday afternoons,
receive Communion
on the tongue
not in palm of hand.

Good girls sew
Power Ranger
Halloween costumes,
bake from scratch,
chaperone first-grade
field trips
to the Baltimore Aquarium.

Good girls don't accelerate
through yellow lights,
don't allow pre-teen sons
to grow hair past shoulders
or listen to Metallica.

Good girls don't long
for afternoons alone,
apartments in the city,
dream jobs on the West Coast,
endless nights
of dancing at concerts,
the smell of men
who are not their husbands.

Ice Jesus

John Hoppenthaler

And then there was Bernie Anderson,
who was my lab partner in high school bio.
He hung out with the heavy metal clique,
so when he etched a Manson-inspired cross
into his forehead we didn't think too much about it.
We kept dissecting worms and frogs and fetal pigs.
He passed me a note once asking if huffing
formaldehyde would get us buzzed. That winter,
because he wanted a stigmata bad but
couldn't will himself one, he broke an icicle
from the eave outside his bedroom window,
pounded it clean through his palm with a rubber
hubcap mallet, and sat at his desk while it melted.
Blood and water ran together everywhere.
When they released him from psychiatric care
he was more elusive than ever, hard
to figure but, sure as shit, his right hand showed
the mark and everyone allowed Bernie a certain
eerie credibility. Later that year he killed himself.
Somewhere—maybe it was an urban legend,
or one of those stories he loved by Poe or De Maupassant,
but he bought a trunk full of frozen blocks
from the Nyack Ice Company when his parents
left for three weeks in Spain, tied a rope
to the back rim of his basketball hoop, placed
the noose around his neck as he stood barefoot
on the stack, handcuffed himself behind his back,
then strangled as ice dissolved beneath his toes.
Had it rained or if, as he must have planned it,
he wasn't found until the dark stain dried
on blacktop, it might be mysterious still
how he died with no chair or ladder there,
and I'm sure he wanted that to be a secret.
He'd think his dying a failure. I wouldn't bring
this up now except for the fact that last week
I went to a friend's wedding. The reception
was at a Holiday Inn in Jersey, and I ditched
into the staging area to bum a choke

from a waiter. We smoked out on the loading
dock and there, on a sheet of plastic behind
the dumpster, a chef was hacking out an ice
sculpture of Jesus for the First Christian Church
of the Second World Dinner/Prayer Meeting
with a chain saw, a chisel, and a rubber mallet.
It was warm for late October. Jesus was sweating—
the chef, too, who was cursing and had just
decided to do the fine cosmetic work
in the walk-in freezer or else, he said, "Christ,
Jesus will end up in the storm drain.
It's a mystery to me," he muttered as he lit
a Lucky Strike, put out the wooden match
with a sizzle on the side of his creation,
"why anyone would want a melting Jesus
in the middle of their savory quiche tarts
and meatballs, but they're paying a freakin' fortune."
Funny how ice dilutes good bourbon just
enough if you drink it with a little urgency.
Let me buy you another;
could I have a cigarette? It's scary
when so much wells up at once.
Got a match? A lighter? Drink up already;
I think our next round is on the tender.

Jungle Gym

Patsy Asuncion

The inner-city beachfront unleashed
gushing fire hydrants mobbed
by neighborhood kids in underwear
for swimsuits, flooded streets

their ocean. They were hard at play
in pavement playgrounds—gangways
for ball games, abandoned cars in weed
lots their forts, and rooftops their hide-

go-seek park. Music was cornered
under street lights by doo-wop dudes
with pompadours who dazzled chicks
with beehives. They be-bopped

together to transistor radio tunes. Slum
kids know no-frill fun. They makeshift,
quick-and-dirty improvise, and dump-
dive prosperity where they find it.

Tell Them You Had a Mole Removed

Julie Hensley

her father said when she worried
what to tell the kids who'd been counting
on her for a group project in AP English
(though, in truth, *Heart of Darkness* made little sense,
bred only damp shadow behind her ribcage—
blind sister to the nausea, that penny-beneath-the-tongue
swirl of saliva that had twice sent her rushing
out of her 9:10 Spanish class).

The same excuse he wrote on the piece of paper
(yellow, lined, torn from the legal pad
where he wrote his own Biology lectures)
which she would unfold for her P.E. teacher later
that afternoon. And Ms. Garrett, who had been
her basketball coach freshman year, back when
Grace still wore braces and white cotton
underwear, would give her a knowing look
before pointing to the wooden bleachers.

But that night, in her lilac-painted bedroom,
when she felt early October through the screen
of her dormer window—
the same one she had lifted
all those summer nights to slide
across the porch roof and
drop herself down,
flip-flops slapping gravel,
thighs warming,
lungs burning as she ran
to where she knew
his truck waited—
she wished for a square of gauze to remove,
black stitches to trace, and later a scar
risen like a white skeleton, something
she might trace again and again.

Gypsy

Dawn Leas

On the first day the corner cafe
props open its front door with a chair,
you know you will survive.

With unzipped windows
and a pushed back sun roof,
you take the slow route between
Wilkes-Barre and Scranton.
A train whistles. Tires speak to pavement
pocked by leftover salt.

The car radio pulls
you deeper
into the '80s
with "Gypsy,"
"Rock with You,"
and "The River."

You pass Ghigarelli's Pizza
and think about the Old Forge
guys you've kissed—
one in the Chuck E. Cheese
parking lot in Dickson City,
the other in a crowded motel room
both of you barely dressed
with bottles dangling from finger tips
during senior week in Wildwood.

The last patches of snow hang
onto Montage Mountain
like acne on the face of a teenager.

You write at every red light,
pass the Taylor Walmart
where you shopped the morning
your water broke with your second son.

You see the house your friend
scraped and painted and decorated

to make just right until her husband left.
The new owners painted over her cherry
red front door with a pea green.

This is the route you drove four times a day
when your boys were an elementary school—
fifteen miles of small towns stitched together
by bars, churches, strip malls, rows of houses
so close they feel each other's breath,
hear the secrets of their neighbors.

The recent past aches like a pulled muscle slow to heal,
a bruise that won't fade,
but this drive is untying the knots.

Crank the volume.
Take a long breath.
Pull to the side of the road
to begin the last line of this poem.
Gather your hair in a loose bun.
Continue to drive as slowly as speed limit will allow.

Words, Words

Sophy Burnham

1. I'm losing my words
Or my mind, one or the other,
Groping for a name, a noun.
The adjective that used to
Leap like a young goat
Off
The cliffs of joy
Onto the page is
Now a stuttered shadow
Of a memory.
They come back, the words return
Drunk and reeling after a night at the bars.
They lurch into the empty streets
bottle-swinging, shout: *Adjacent*
Tapas! Ecru!
Daisy Miller!
Awake in bed I grind my teeth
Helpless against the green glass
Shattering on the dawn curbs
Curfew! Origami!
When what I needed was now hours gone.
They slink off laughing like felons
On the prowl.

2. I dream how when I die the words will all come back
Falling in apple blossom blessings
Paper whirligigs
Floating, falling through the silence
Majestically
White cranes curving
To my tongue
Taut and tangy to the touch.
They'll flap one indolent wing
To keep aloft
Swoop, settle on my scorched skin
Like burning kisses:
Affectionate, disorderly, extravagant
All the polysyllabic Latinates commingling

With rough Saxon sounds
As brash and coarse as crows.
They trudge through the forests of our history
Swords swinging, hacking out ransom,
wreck, match, milk, muck, reek,
crackle and *ax, barn* and *cairn.*
They are homey and redolent with the smell of dirt
or death. And we find
Chinese, Spanish, Arabic,
Yiddish, each word
Attesting to the endless
Migrations of humankind.

3. In my dream the words snow
Silently from gunmetal skies, drift in piles
And twirl light wind-whipped powder-soft,
These carriers of the fierce music
Of my life.
Buckled and booted for war
The huntsman's horn, the screech of wheel,
Laments of loneliness and love.
They are choral bells pealing forth their
Hope faith fears.
They are canticles to
The times
We've known before
This time round.
In my dream
I wonder if it's words I'll miss
The most
When I depart
Or whether words will wing
In whatever heaven I'm assigned.
I'd even want another incarnation
Here if I could hear
Words tumbling from your
Beautiful sweet mouth, pouring
From the bellows of your throat.

First Thing

Ed Zahniser

in the nursing home I'm going to remake my reputation
a human gumbo thick as rich soup
thick as the limestone-bottom marsh outside town
where wild animals flaunt the norm
by outliving their own fertility with the precise
and tender geometry of desire while in town
some randy pedant mimics Roman poet Catullus
love-struck with others' scatology not to mention
spontaneous overflow of powerful feelings thought long
and deeply enough to be-weep with God all our faults
like accountants who don't take vacations or sick leave
then turn out to be embezzlers and of course
we poets also steal some lines but the difference
is if they ever need them again we can and do
give them right back

Late Offer: In Decima

Linda Dove

I do not want to be your wife.
Yes, you do shoot a good line.
But, with respect, I decline.
Me? Risk galloping off a cliff
In such messy waters of life—
At my age! My bad, I confess.
Compromise would cause such stress—
Cash, TV remote, clean shirt.
Worse—which side of the bed? Learn to flirt
Again? No! I can't acquiesce!

But what if I put on the brake?
Perhaps, a nuptial agreement
to which I'm sure you could consent?
How about we both give and take?
Don't grin. You'll give me stomach ache!
Now see, keep your own bank account:
Have your own bed, if that's paramount.
In return, just cook me hot stew,
Oh! And I want meat I can chew
Oh! And I hate my knife to be blunt.

Well, now it's my turn to be clear.
I see I'll have to be brutal.
Your offer to me is futile.
Late coupling can be just veneer.
Living alone I hold quite dear.
You need a good maid, a good cook,
and—perhaps—a new pocketbook.
Are you clear that's my attitude?
You're a handsome dude, but don't let's feud.
I won't hang myself on your hook.

Math for Girls Counts

Patsy Asuncion

Before they were great-great-grandmothers, they stood
in lines for singular equality, for one scale blind
to gender, creed or color. But, their right

to vote was delayed until 1920—144 years after
propertied White men, 51 years after Black men,
as if women were mere household amenities
used as conveniences.

The vote hoped to move the line closer
to a public voice in fiscal and sexual values,
but it took sixteen more years to change
birth control methods from *obscene*

to legal mail (hidden in plain brown envelopes)
to head-of-the-household husbands,
a married man the only
Good Housekeeping Seal of Approval.

Connecticut's 1965 defeat freed the pill
only for the sanctified wedded. I remember
unmarried, pregnant girls,
shamed and blamed for bad choices,
while boys were just being boys.

The 1982 ERA defeat subtracted sixty years
of female rights. One hundred years since suffrage,
fifteen states still have not ratified ERA,
now a dusty museum piece.

Defeat meant I had no credit, no bank account,
no property without my husband's name, addressed as
Mrs. John Doe, my first name unimportant,
a nondescript dustpan beneath spousal steps.

The recent Hobby Lobby Act fractionalized
1973's *Roe vs. Wade* by granting corporations
religious rights to reduce reproductive choice,
lost winnings by poker cheats.

Despite the centuries-old male monopoly,
women have done the math—
equal means equal, not less than.

Back Talk

Patsy Asuncion

When I was a kid, I could scoot around
on my mental roller skates to any city block
in Chicago and speak the language of the
hood, the words which colored that culture.

I spoke enough Polish to order the best
pierogis or tell off a punk Polack. I used my
basic Spanish to shop at the local Puerto Rican
mercado and Italian to flirt with cute *Dego* boys.

Foreign phrases common to these old neighborhoods
stuck with me—*vanffancul,* (with rude arm gestures),
jak się masz, dónde está el baño, dziękuję, ¿Qué pasa?
They flew effortlessly off my tongue.

The years have now confused my links to language
with detours to other definitions and passing phrases,
with traffic delays around newly-constructed words.
Old lingo now lingers on street corners I can't find.

Building the Future

Jen Karetnick

We told the city
it was a garden shed,
stocked up on can openers
and machetes, steel siding
with a guarantee to last
the lifespan of a marmoset.

We told the city
it was a tiki hut,
learned how to harvest
bamboo and cut rattan,
plait the finest tossa jute
and also eat it in soup.

We told the city
it was a tree house,
sunk pillars next to
each mango in its patient
position leftover
from the plantation days,

trunks set into formation
like clarinets in a marching band.
We said we would evacuate
along the prescribed path,
without our pets
but with our children

and important papers,
enough belongings
for a day or two
in the school gym.
We never told the city
kelong, pang uk, palfito,

heliotrope, stilt house,
not because the city
told us they didn't have
permits for the end
of dry-footed days
but because when it came

time to hoist it like a flag
and follow suit,
we had already found
our hot, briny resolve
while the city was still
looking for a problem.

A cup of coffee, a cigarette, and an attempt to read the day's newspaper

John McKenna

again the city summer heat leapt and lurched from sewer drain and subway from corner and curb from fire escape—where there was none —street tar and rubber searing up and out of each crack and crevice while the sweat of strangers passed in drip smudge and bump from arm and shoulder to arm and shoulder at corners and in crowds the quick pace of Manhattan slowed not yet among the movements there were those whose wasted and warn wander was visible sticky skin and denim sundress and shades heat crackle colour collage snaking and twisting whirling and writhing in and out of avenue sidewalks crowded with shadows morphed exaggerated elongated gaudy the grotesque extension of bodies the labored pace of the people wearing laundry white cotton ruined yellow—the soil of sweat urine yellow cabs darting as humans dive into the pedestrian surf into the street from crumbling cement corners breasts young and old alike, bounce drag or dangle beneath tee-shirt and peasant blouses the requisite pack of punkers—walk'n hard talk'n loud and doing "A"-jack-shit chain smoking and laughing and hiding loudly in pegged jeans and god-on-fire combat boots and the march of Brooks Brothers clientele with suit jacket perfectly poised over a shoulder the hard heavy procession of the immigrant elderly women pulling and women pushing small thin chrome and black wheeled carts to and from the market and again the Israeli and Persian women beautiful born of heat and fire cool and graceful and flowing they alone glide past fast through the troubled clogged push stop stagger halt begin again of Manhattan

Me stupid

Sophy Burnham

When me come out weak thin starve
four pound small by measurement,
say me owl-eyed, silent, say me carve
in color cocoa, say day by day me sent
them marvel still me alive.
Not till later school, me nine,
it defect show, they say 'count of no give
answer like they others shine,
me stupid, bullied dirt thrown, hit
then rape in playground, then times more,
and more cuz of me no fit
for better say they boy hitch jeans me too sore
walk weep by me lone, me mamma high
me papa gone. Fourteen now and baby nigh

belly-big, me eat, want feed she, and when me lie
in bed me whisper to she, sing, me sigh
how she gon be so pretty, yes, have faculties
read write be smart not deaf like me.

Equinox

At the Mayan temple El Castillo at Chichen Itza, dusk before spring and fall equinox, shadows cast by the setting sun form a serpent—Kulkulkan a god in the Mayan cosmos—down the steps of the temple.

Susan Notar

The equinox draws near
our serpiente can almost taste
the light's sleepy rays before the horizon
hides them in its pocket. O light lick el Castillo tonight

we agreed once to meet
on a different continent every equinox

O Kulkulkan unfurl
each inch of your emerald ebony cerulean
coils. Bless our cacao avocados, mais
lick el Castillo tonight

we agreed once to meet
on a different continent every equinox
and kiss in starlight

O serpiente el Castillo rises above the jungle
each step a day of the year we would climb
feel the smooth cool stone
on our calloused hot feet
if we could but only priests may

we agreed once to meet
on a different continent
every equinox and kiss in starlight
but you were gone

O
O serpiente

Time Zone

Judy Kronenfeld

7:59 p.m.: a woman in a Cairo room
with fifteen-foot decaying ceilings of colonial
splendor gazes out her window at the neighboring rooftop
squatters, and in the distant Cities of the Dead,
Cities of the Living, a lump of flesh
in black robes grayed by dust scuttles
from cenotaph to cenotaph. In Bucharest's
blue dusk lingering, a queue
quietly forms for bread before a milky-white-lit
bakery, shadowed by the black behemoth
of a cement-slab hotel; in rain-smudged
Istanbul, someone weeps into linens
smelling like damp dust; in smoggy Athens
near the Agora, a gypsy child
hangs on a tourist's hand.

And here, and there, beyond the glistening districts
a little more ancient soot soft as fur gathers on windowsills,
on crumbling steps, tattered laundry stiffens a little more
against chipped facades, and the solitary comers
and goers turn down narrow streets,
on an eternal circuit from the newsstand
to the market—a half-liter milk to chill in the rusty refrigerator
as long as there's power, an apple and pear
for the bowl in the dark tiny kitchen, yellow shades
drawn against summer.

8:01 and the woman lifts her gaze
from the window, the black-robed form
unwraps a bowl of koshary, the queue
grows longer by three; the weeper
gets up from her bed; the tourist
shrugs the gypsy off. Now ghosts
of all who've ever come to evening—
under roofs or in the open air—
in the cities of this time zone, gather.
In my own room, some press
against my shoulder, trying to scan the news

of dearth and deluge; some watch
juice drip from the knife
that peels the pear.

November Picnic at Kohl's Department Store

Ed Zahniser

Today Kohl's sounds like a front for sex trafficking.
The loudspeaker voice keeps coming on to solicit:
"Boys, please. Boys please." Which reminds me: I forgot
to go back to the Keurig coffee demo where earlier
I showed the salesperson how to turn on the machine.
Even then its read-out screen said NOT READY.
"I'll come back," I said. Now I haven't, distracted
by such overt sex-trafficking. In Customer Service
the Customer Servant tells another staffer how
yesterday her young son told her *I can't hear you!*
I turned my ears off. A young male clerk bops by
and tells the Customer Servant "Today's going fast,"
as though maybe the winter solstice is imminent,
but I assume he just looks forward to his workday's
end. Gerald Stern, whose *Paradise Poems* I'm reading,
would remark how this young fellow reminds him of Ovid
—not that Stern ever met Ovid or wants you to think
he did—and except for *The Metamorphoses* I can't recall
much of Ovid except his book was not about caterpillars
turning into butterflies. Stern's allusion eludes me like
a butterfly or, if I concentrate long enough, a caterpillar.

Now I'm back in Customer Service in a chair, drinking
Italian Dark Roast Keurig Coffee as I notice *mi sposa*
has already gone through the checkout line. So next
we're sitting on a bench outside Kohl's front door
picnicking on homemade sandwiches we packed.
We suspect the patron passers-by have cartoon bubbles
above their heads that read "Must both be retired," but
suddenly I drown in remembering what depressed me
about college was how even your closest best classmates
that you'd grown as close to as I'm sitting to *mi sposa* now
—how they kept walking out of your life never to return
ever as though each graduation ejects the co-pilot seat.
But then the Italian bread of my sandwich brought me
in for a soft landing, if only because I was surprised
how firm the crust was and how maybe I'd be better off
with thicker skin myself for a November picnic at Kohl's.

I've hardly unfastened my seatbelt when a couple walks
by with zero eye contact and both cartoon bubbles blank.

My Secret Poems

Amie Sharp

It's too bad you've only these
to read—too many words,
images limp and tired, beggaring
the depths of my vision.

In my secret files, there are fugues
of astonishing perception
and grace. And they're *funny*—
you'd just die if you could read

the one about the spaceship
and the man with the orange hat.
None of these pathetic scribblings there.
No, my secret poems raise us all

onto a pedestal chiseled
with the purest longing. There
I have found the way to talk to God
and not stammer in His presence.

But the moment I show anyone,
it's as if someone else has taken
my words and translated them all
into a language I don't understand.

Only in America

Heather Banks

Only in America—
A Persian takes my order for a Greek salad and shouts in Spanish to the cook.

Only in America—
The neighborhood pizza joint with a brick oven now serves Tandoori chicken as well, and the cooks at the Caspian Cafe are from Vietnam.

Only in America—
The landscape crew of Guatemalans has a supervisor from Bosnia.

Only in America—
My newest neighbors arrived because they were suddenly on the wrong side—one in Ethiopia and one in Madagascar.

Only in America—
My eye doctor from India is a neighbor of my dentist from Bangladesh.

Only in America—
My grandparents from Scotland saw me marry a Taiwanese
and now my son's main squeeze is the sensei girl next door.

Only in America.

Invitation to sing a song in French: *Tout va très bien, Madame la Marquise*

Albert Russo

There is a French song
entitled *Tout va très bien, Madame la Marquise*
which is at once ironic and quite funny
every day, over the phone
La Marquise asks her butlers
what is new in the castle
"the barn has burnt down," he says,
then intones "apart from that everything
is hunky-dory, Madame."
"hello, hello, my good man", she inquires,
"tell me how things are today,"
"your favorite mare has died in the flames,"
he responds, "but apart from that
everything is hunky-dory, Madame"
and the story goes on during a whole week
until the castle itself and the stable lie in ashes
so that La Marquise has lost her beautiful property
at the end, she learns that all this has happened
because her husband, the Marquis, has committed suicide
and by doing so, set fire to both the castle and the stable
La Marquise is, of course,
totally distraught and out of her mind
still the butlers end with the same sentence:
"*A part cela, Madame la Marquise,*
tout va très bien, tout va très bien."

Once Upon

George Perreault

It begins like any legendary story, those
tales you learned in school, ancient Greeks
or some medieval forest, emerald grottoes

dripping with fairies, goblins or some such,
a little house, that girl with the golden eyes,
and potions, always something you've eaten—

an innocent wanderer, a couch, some flirting
and then she's flying into the kitchen to stir
or add a pinch or this or that, the air aromatic,

the table groaning with temptation and he's
inhaling *alambre,* morsels of *carne guisada,*
or whole mouthfuls of *queso flameado,*

he's spellbound by *calabacitas con puerco,*
undone by *huachinango a la Veracruzana,*
and now enthralled, he offers everything,

fortunes exchanged with she who can barely
boil water (her sister busy at the hidden stove)
a door closes, and Golden-Eyes turns the key.

Papá's War Song

—for my son, Joaquín

Seth Michelson

Joaquín: bright blue starlight
traveled centuries
to sing from your eyes,
born in the flooded junction
of the Río de la Plata
and the Los Angeles River,
mestizo: part gaucho,
part L.A. Dodger, red hair,
dulce de leche skin, a Latin
heartbeat: pum-PUM.
So please hear me, Quinito,
when I say look both ways in life
then look some more,
because the local mobs,
O, they will come:
chanting beneath burning pitchforks,
and they'll forgive
nothing as they strike
to take it all from you, mi Quinito,
against which your best chance
is a quick song
and a hard right hook.

Semana Santa

Susan Notar

In the Yucatan lime, *limon*, is tangy
and squeezed on everything:
mango, piña, pollo.
Lime, salt, and the sea
the air redolent of all three.

She lets the waves of the mar caribe
buoy her to the surface
the sun bring her back from the depths
where she'd recently been dwelling.

She is imagining him
of pulling their bodies apart,
after, in the heat of Yucatecan afternoons.

Or maybe it would rain
they would embrace in it
on the balcony, next to the hammocks
he would take a handful of it
rinse the blood from her lip
where he'd kissed her a little too hard.

She would withstand it
without complaint
knowing that the line
between pleasure and pain
was as thin as a Mayan child's hair
and just as full of history.

Golden Dragon Babies

William Sypher

From Ho Chi Minh City to Hanoi
it was the Year of the Dragon
and not just any fire breather
but a golden one, the kind
that fires the mind
and stirs the loins
once in 2000 years:
a bi-millennial dragon.

Months before this golden year
all over Viet Nam,
couples coupled
with clear intent:
a child born in
this auspicious year
would roll in wealth
glow with health
such is the power of myth.
They labored not in vain
nine percent more babies
had emerged this year:
golden dragon babies

Their parents were ecstatic,
a joy not shared by bureaucrats
who clucked in dark dismay.
Their plan to stem the rate of birth,
which had been working admirably,
was now in disarray.

Some St. George or
East Asian Beowulf
had to slay this dragon
that was inspiring procreation.
The Population Ministry,
short on creativity—

unlike the fecund couples—

turned to advertisers.

On Tae Win Do Street,
Madison Avenue of Hanoi,
dragon slaying began in earnest.
Someone proposed Golden Dragon condoms
"for peak satisfaction."
This fooled no one,
sales were slack.
It wasn't satisfaction
couples sought, but
bi-millennial babies,
Golden Dragon babies.

Astronomers weighed in
with calculators and a grin
trying to hoodwink citizens.
"The year is not what you think;
it's not the year 2000 yet,"
because a Pope in far-off Italy
once goosed the calendar
when such an act was not so serious
or ripe with portent.

This astronomical sleight-of-hand
worked no better than
the Golden Dragon condoms brand.
Lusty hopes beyond the reach
of bureaucratic hacks.
beyond the point of turning back.
Coitus interruptus? Hmmm,
a dreary, dusty Latin phrase
Turn over, dear,
there'll be no turning back.

The only hope it seemed
was to redefine the Golden Dragon,
to dim some of its luster.

For this, wordmeisters were at hand:
"All that glitters is not gold"
was their first attempt that bombed.
"Do not exalt the golden idol."
Wrong religion; same result.
"Gilding the lily," tepid, too,
and what could be more irrelevant
than the fabled golden rule:
When they were already
doing unto others . . .
That was the rub.
Clichés drawn against clichés:
"Takes two to tango,"
but two's were dancing,
oh, were they dancing.

Then one linguist quipped,
"We must fight fire with fire;
we'll counter superstition
with freshly minted myth like:
"Designer Golden Dragon babies,
conceived by plan
instead of accident,
reap not gold but hardship."
Yes, that should work.
among a people wed to superstition.

These warning words
sped around the land
printing presses ran red hot
billboards erected on the spot
newspapers, handbills filled the streets
hourly warnings: radio and TV.
The Population Ministry
panted in anticipation
that its campaign would work.

Then some wag

eager to re-gird the loins
spoke out against this One Year Plan,
called it calendar genocide:
monkey business,
a sacrilegious mixing of
the year of the Monkey with
the year of the lustrous Dragon.
"The Golden Dragon reigns supreme;
the Golden Dragon is not gone—breed on,"
he shouted in Khe San Square,
before men dressed liked citizens
ushered him somewhere
his rants would not be heard,
but they had been heard.

Now all across the land
from Ho Chi Minh City to Hanoi
couples are back at work,
the birth rate's soaring,
dour bureaucrats reduced to
marking days off calendars.

Undone by the Khe San shout,
myth and passion have won out,
and Viet Nam will have to live
with far too many
freshly minted dragon babies.

A Night of Anapests

Linda Dove

Like a flashlight through fog on and off
irritating my internal clock
and depriving my brain of repose
was my plan to arise before dawn
to arrive for the flight in good time
to check in with my bags and avoid
middle seats and the toilets and galley
leaving plenty of time after that
to go early through passport control
remove shoes and ear-rings and Iphone
make security easy and look
for my gate to check that my flight
number 10 still takes off from gate 8
international terminal D
accessed only on shuttle C2
and is not on the list of delays
or much worse has been cancelled for storms
or mechanical problems of some sort
in which case I will lose my connection
in Atlanta well known too for delays
and who knows when on earth I'll arrive
in Japan and bow to my hosts
in polite dignified greeting.

Arising before dawn
spilt my coffee
groped for car keys
drove two hours
on dark roads
found departures
but no agents
at any desk
much too soon
to check in.

Hard Bench. Doze Upright. Think in Spondees.

West-Bound Flowers

John Berry

While walking some miles
on a busy road
with a protest sign
advancing the merits of *Love*
and *Peace*

you will notice, first of all,
a preponderance of plastic.
It will be as though the rains which fell
last week hurtled out of the sky
in twelve ounce drops,
leaving the empty shells
of their skins lying about in the gutter.

You will encounter at least one solitary shoe
from the foot of a child,
and you will wonder if it had flown
from the half-open window of a mini-van
in the midst of a tantrum
or mischief or joy.

You will see an empty, cheap, cotton glove
you will be certain someone forgot
with its mate on the bumper or bed
of a truck.

From a distance, snakes will appear in your path,
turning to vulcanized ribbons of rubber
as you draw near.

And stranger things—blue, broken
umbrella handles, empty picture frames,
magazines you will be surprised to see
are still in print.

And the common—a million last drags smoked
and tossed as if both man and woman alike
had seeded the un-furrowed row of the shoulder

with embers of anger.

And finally the corpses.
The mummified pelts and bones
of sudden sure death;
even the skunks robbed of their virulent presence,
dry as the desolate grass.

Your hair and clothes will stink from the fumes,
and when at last you have occasion to speak
your voice will be raw, coated with soot.

You will have left bits of yourself behind
with the fast-food wrappers
and aluminum cans.

You will be bruised where the sign has rubbed your collar
in the hurricane force of the semis assaulting
the west-bound flowers.

Fracturing Light on Water

Trevor Tingle

Nine suns ripple on the lake,
ten flat top live oaks under an olive sky,
and a baby blue '67 Impala with the door ajar.

Nine toes play with pebbles below.
The autumn light weaves through your unwashed hair,
and it's hard to dismiss the sun's accuracy.

You are not walking away.

Knotted bits of scab drift off
and settle with the rest of the detritus.
Your mind wanders, and you want to wander too,
but you don't know where.

You find yourself in the driver's seat
imagining your foot on the accelerator.
You find more comfort in the white noise between radio stations
than the stations themselves so you turn the thing off.
The cicadas sing of the distance from here to home.

If you leave the car any longer they'll tow.

You sigh, shut the door and close your eyes.
Your nostrils fill with smoke and leather smiles,
the smell of whiskers brushing your face before bed.

Your foot is sore.
Your hands are heavy.
You're not going to make it.

Airplanes in the Sky

John Most

pen strikes become
questions
you'd never ask the night,
breathless. 'how do
you ever know if cool-
to-the-touch London is
London, if separation
is yellow thread
or finality?'

to resume means
passengers circle
their destination.

it's diving into a pond,
green algae pulled from
black water. as
lilies are flowers,

a postcard she sent
from Venice falls from
the pages.

Steel Season

Michael Waterson

Black water of three rivers lies below,
defined by city lights.
I'm flying back to coal barges, still there,
floating invisible in the dark. Banking,
the plane flies on over Moon Run dairies,
blue runway lights. I am eager to inhale
brittle air and see my breath blow into a blizzard.

Japanese clouds ride the jet stream into Napa,
drop yellow bursts of mustard between bare vines,
gnarled ideograms, black and dripping with rain,
unpronounceable words you walk among,
that could you sound out, get your tongue around,
would tell life stories in an utterance.
From pampas grass to eucalyptus trees,
fault zone transplants thrive.

I have forgotten
how crowded hills bristle with trees,
how stubborn shadows cling to drifts;
how red brick houses shoulder the wind,
while salt and cinders assault the shoe leather
of hunched foot traffic that never looks up.

'Winter's steel season,' old mill hunkies say,
'Furnace work needs cold tempering.' They drink
Iron City Beer and talk of the days of black snow
before the stacks stopped smoking around the clock
with the stench of rotten eggs. When cars were steel
and real men gladly worked three shifts and spit
on the grave of Henry Clay Frick.

It all comes back: old fear and anger banked
with the Bessemers that blasted night skies
with a false, flickering dawn that still burns,
only now in the slow, cold fire of rust.
Slag piles surrender ghosts grudgingly
to ragweed, dandelion, and the drizzle

and grit of one more spring.
Allegheny and Monongahela meld in my blood.
The first bitter breath remembers me.

Clouds as Links and Diviners

"If you look at clouds long enough, they will give you the answers."
—Mma Precious Ramotswe, owner of Ladies No. 1 Detective Agency
in Botswana, quoting her late father, farmer Obed Ramotswe

Heather Banks

A friend on a farm in another state lives close to the land,
posts daily Facebook photos of moon and dawn most days.
Such variety of golden tints and silver tinsel
or flagrant flamingo of bursting rays amazes.

In my last house, I too saw dawns
framed by tree tops behind my home.
But here, the woods and others' hilltop houses
steal those early views from me.

Now I see sunsets' wide riots from my back deck
and wonder what others from past decades of my life
see as they rise early or come home late
where they make music in the Dakotas,
teach Chinese at Berkeley,
tend orphans in Haiti
or a small farm in Normandy.

Cumulus, nimbus, cirrus, stratus clouds—
skies change it seems to us at whim.
Brilliant blue without a blotch emblazoned,
can shift to solid grey and grim.
Myriad puffs whoosh or gambol, float slowly on,
then threaten storm with grisly tinge.

In our todays and in every gaze,
each surely sees quite different clouds.
In them, we find a moment's message
or lesson learned as age and life and latitude vary,
near or in farthest hemisphere
where even the stars are different.

Skiing Barefoot over the Wrecks

I came to see the damage that was done
and the treasures that prevail.—Adrienne Rich

Jen Karetnick

The trick is to ease
the hold on the handle,
don't allow knuckles
to knot like curtains
over a rod braced
between the shoulders
of a double-hung window.

I lie back in the water
to start, feet meeting
hands greeting rope
at mid-thigh,
ears immersed
in the amniotic bouillon,
listening only
to the heartbeat of the ocean
as if there is no other
world, was never
another world,
below me.

I give a thumbs-up
to the driver of the boat
who will ease me,
feeding me out
from the other
end of this cord,
before pulling taut
and I resist the drag.

This is not labor.
The spray claps my face
like applause, each drop
one of approval,
and while the wind
in my hair is generated,

the source of its power
is not man-drilled,
not a god
but the childish,
oblivious sun, who cares
nothing about what goes
on underneath it,
about what it can
or cannot dry up.

And I am up,
riding the weedy surface
on the flats of my feet,
over flooded, flattened
houses whose ghosts
billow under my soles,
blowing up
into a white-tipped
wake that my heels
zip through, sun-bruised,
mango-cured, tough
as sharks. Still

they are spiny
sea urchins, these spirits
of screened-in Florida
rooms where pianos used
to wait for hands reluctant
as fire in wet saw grass,
underutilized kitchens
owned by diners
who preferred restaurants,
bedrooms that saw nothing
more than too little
sleep, achieved
with the open mouth

of the dead
and disrespectful.

Now the Dade County
pine floors, once
so prized and polished
or scarred by termites
and the careening
claws of dogs have rotted,
either way, into driftwood.
Coral has gone back
to coral. The dogs
who have been left to us
wear lifejackets
and the dead live again,
reefs for grouper
and parrotfish.

If I look down
into the foundations
of heartbreak and recovery,
epiphanies and realizations,
culminations and failures,
I, too, will fall,
forgetting all fundamentals,
unable to tuck and roll,
my external walls
shooting nails
in every direction
to wash up later
on the beaches like teeth,
each room of my body
cartwheeling into disrepair.

So I keep my eyes
forward, toward
what would be
the ponytails of palms

and the canopies of mangos
if those trees still rooted
here, and my grip
casual, thumbs lined up
next to index fingers
as if on a golf club,
holding on
to nothing too dear
too dearly.

The Rose City of Petra

Albert Russo

Behind the mount of Hor where Aaron is buried
in the Valley of Moses the Nabateans

built palaces of splendor carved in the rock
lofty canyons scraping the sky of a

limpid translucent blue Surrounded

by the desert a thousand walls

sprout in phantasmal hues from sand pink to coal brown

through all the shades of coral

defying the laws of gravity Walking

in the narrow corridors that separate them

you feel at once dwarfed and

exhilarated imagining you are
the emissary of a foreign court
awaited by the King of Petra

And the towering walls
stand guard, protecting you
all the way to the palace
Then all of a sudden
as if emerging from a dream
between the cracks of a gorge
a doric column appears
holding parts of a monumental crown
An ethereal silence sets in
and you slow your pace
lest the miracle fades into a mirage
the air is brimming with sand particles
yet you fear that if you remain still
you will be turned into a pillar of salt

like Lot's wife in the Bible
your feet shuffle on the pebbly ground
and the crunching sound fills you with terror

then in a surge of courage
you slip out of the crack
and face the majestic facade
of the golden Khaznah

The Minister's Last Morning

"He asked me 'Why?' I just said I was sorry."—Mary Winkler

Amie Sharp

In Tennessee, morning clouded. Gray light fell
as the dirt-water day began its crawl, crib to tomb.
But whatever the secrets, the house can't tell.

The young wife lifted the shotgun, loaded with shell.
Blank as a child, she'd tell the court she felt a strange boom
as the morning clouded, and gray light fell

through the ruffled bedrooms the girls knew so well.
How much did they hear as his red back bloomed?
Whatever the secrets, the house can't tell.

His parents keep the girls, but fear soon she'll
walk—a brief sentence gaveled in the courtroom.
When the morning clouded and gray light fell,

that she'd endured forced sex, pain towering well
beyond rage against the man who was her groom—
whatever the secrets, the house can't tell.

She buckled the girls in, slammed the door like a cell.
The phone ripped free, he finished bleeding in their room.
Outside, the morning clouded and gray light fell
on whatever secrets the house can't tell.

Remembering James Wright

Michael Waterson

I see you in a coal barge tugged
upriver to Wheeling, or
tossing back boilermakers, spirit of Li Po
possessing you, ruptured night watchman
on the next barstool.

Now you mull varieties,
subtleties of hangovers,
reworking a poem about wasted lives as
the branch outside your window breaks
into blossom.

Born a hundred slag piles east,
a generation later,
I too longed to stoke the heart's open hearth,
forge song from labors' sweat-soaked oaths,
commune with the ancient
Chinese governor stepping over
a mud puddle.

I too longed to embrace the moon
reflected in your Ohio.

Hands with Grapes

Georgia O'Keefe, 1921 Photo by Alfred Steiglitz
Susan Notar

In sepia tones
O'Keefe's fingers are splayed on a leaf
plucking grapes
spider-like in their agility.
Sense her impatience
at posing for her lover
while he clicked frame after frame
until he found
just the right one.
This was before O'Keefe left
full-time for the American southwest
yet in the stretch of her fingertips
you can sense her yearning
for what lies beyond the frame
what she'd seek to capture.

Elvis in Hell

Michael Waterson

Even on days he is condemned to shake
off dusty death and rise again to make
another roadside cameo before a
white-line-wired rigger highballing Peoria,
or a spectral reflection in the Tulsa window-
shopping reverie of a football widow,

even then, in those moments he is risen
under the sun, his soul remains imprisoned
in a velvet painting in El Paso,
a sequined T-shirt in a Boardwalk casino,
a Nashville plaster coin bank statuette.

These haunts new and old render no release
for a U.S. male of the old stamp from the net
of impersonators, harpies of regret
drawling old songs that scald like bacon grease;

offer no freedom, sweet and redeeming,
like in those golden olden hound dog days
on the flat-bed stages of state fair midways,
girls in cotton dresses crying and screaming
as the music just erupted from within
like gospel grace pouring down from heaven.

No more: the ghost gig is mere dumb show
and stygian nights flash neon agony.
For he is not the hot act Down Below.
The King is dead; no headliner, he,
in sold-out rooms on the infernal Strip;
just a has-been warm-up for the big marquee,
the grinning boss of Mephistopheles,
who sets 'em howling with a quivering lip and a quip:
Take my dignity . . . Please!

On Russian Hill

John McKenna

I.
there you find yourself

yourself
if you know to know

there again
beneath the new chrome metallic glistening night
breathing
healing
heaven
whisper and wishing

rubbing your hands together near the trash can fire
quick to coat pockets a Chesterfield and a Zippo
a favorite gift to you from you to you from then
of once ago pawn shop
if you had only been James and knew who Uncle Benny was
and why congratulations were in order years and years and years ago
wondering again about them now

you offer and share a smoke with the new old new old always
 friends
brothers and sisters
listening to the pop-fizz-crackit-spurff-sssnap as wood shatters
burning within the trashcan
casting hurling—birthing new stars straight and sometimes
sideways up and out
to brief fly flight
and exhaust on sidewalk, collar and cuff
of this
this little huddled new-made tribe

II.
two bottles pass around
arriving to you at the same time
rare
the wine is Red Red Red Rioja and Malbec

you slug and pull from one and then the others as new wine is made
there in your mouth
across your lips and tongue and throat
and warm deep deep
while spilling just a bit
laughing
not alone
and more laughter
passing with joy and certain generous grateful hold hand
pass to another each other

sharing
folks just wanting to stand a little closer
hug and kiss a little longer

as night drapes
drenches and drinks us
christening and anointing each

in
silver
platinum
perfection

above apricot and wild-rose-colored fire
made in tribute

and soon and so and so

III.
are you in the Bronx tonight, sleeping in Spanish Harlem,
Sunnyside—maybe?
down on Astoria Boulevard, the East Side or praying away in
Camden

Or have you flown flew further West still
and again Chicago, again East St. Louis or again
there rising on the mountain

on that great gray and green garbed Denver?

have you laid your blanket down in the Mission are you there in Fillmore?

Just look a ways up

North

Do you see that new fire?

We are waiting for you on Russian Hill

and no one is going anywhere
until you and Dawn breathes please kiss us

not goodbye
not so long
but only good God Gaia morning

and then we'll wander down to along the wharf
and find coffee
and share read the newspaper together

quiet and in Love
each one of us with the other

and know this

Diabetes

Amie Sharp

My mother pricks her finger. Dinner's almost
ready—halftime, our team losing again,
and now her rosemary potatoes will be our solace.
For the fourth time today, she tests her blood.

My mother loves football and Westerns,
James Garner as Maverick. Years after a virus
ambushed her pancreas, thousands of injections,
she wears an insulin pump, and while it works

she's a classic movie savant. Give her any
character actor, Sydney Greenstreet, say—
she can list his roles. But then her sugar drops,
her blue eyes haze, she casts her filmy mind

around for what she needs . . . orange juice . . .
some jelly beans. She's told me of a man
from my Tennessee hometown, who left
the hospital after his amputation to hobble

through the front door of Allison's Restaurant.
A helpless waitress brought him apple pie
and watched as he ate the whole thing,
gambling his very blood on its sweetness.

Just sick of it, my mother guessed,
the sugar scales that never stay
balanced. Now she squeezes a glossy
disc onto a strip, deciphers numbers.

She doesn't mention the ocean of these
red droplets she's measured. Because
we need her, she knows what she has to do
again and again and again and again.

Bee Weight

Patricia Gray

Once, in Szechwan Province,
pear trees bore so plenteously
that insects buzzed round
in drunken bliss and birds
swooped in staggering loops
as ripe pears fell, fermenting
in an ecstasy of rot.

But that time is gone.
Honeybee hives are deserted,
pollen left untouched, pear honey
unmade, and from this sudden
vanishing, humans have become bees,
inventing a birdfeather brush
fastened to a rod and dipped
into pollen to tickle each opulent
blossom like the dry kiss of an old man,
causing the blooms to shudder, and
enough pears to ripen to export
for fresh pear syrup and wine.

But in my small field this spring,
honeybees skip from bean flower
to clover, murmuring and wriggling
their pollen-clad legs, quivering
their wings so lightly and quickly
that blossoms tremble and bounce
as bee weight lifts—rising
for farther sweet regions.

Better Seeds

Hiram Larew

Looking up seems early
I'm going to slip outside as soon as
        sprigs poke and fences shine
Scout about until you wave me in for breakfast
I'm going to lean into my wishes
Because this is the nickel time of spring
When legs seem longer.

There are better ways of learning
Ways as ready as your bird box
There are better people
Ones who get polished by the wind
And there are better seeds
The kind that wait a year or two.

But it's hard to wait when everything is curling
When time slips through curtains to let us know
That this chance is more than our pillows
It's quicker than that
It's kind of like our neighbor
Who slides a box of kale starts
Onto the porch first thing
Chuckling not to wake us.

Breech

Steven Knepper

A farmer knows the point where prayer
And blasphemy are one—*My God, My God*—
The shepherd-psalmist's cry of dereliction.
A windstorm flattens out his corn, a chainsaw
Bites into his firstborn's leg, the well
Goes dry in August's drought.

The night my father breathes such words his lips
Are beaded up, his cotton shirt soaked through,
His arm a swollen mass of blood and slime
From failed attempts to push, to turn, to pinch
The breeched calf's legs, a stubborn inch's task.
Frustration mounts as minutes turn to hours
Without the necessary shift, the cow
No longer bellowing. Her head hangs low.
Our neighbor puts his shoulder in her side
To keep her upright in the narrow stall.
The pulling chains lie useless on the floor.
I dab a towel across my father's face
And keep the water hot, add iodine
To crudely sterilize. The slug of brown
Uncoils its tendrils in the steaming pail.
Despite myself I think about the day
He had to shoot a spraddled cow to ease
Her misery. She was a heavy milker,
A thousand dollar cow. My mother cried.
My father's eyes were wild as he returned
The rifle to the rack, went back to work.
Damn it all. He sinks against the blocks.
My God, My God. He pumps his arm, exhales
The words, then stumbles up again to try
To wrench a miracle into the world.

Ambrosia

Julie Hensley

The first thing he made her was a rocker.
For the frame: worm wood,
a maple found fallen on a hunting trip,
branches big around as a human thigh
he dragged out of Runkles Gap.
The sawing he arranged at a family mill near Luray—
he traded a rifle for that lumber, dried sweet
in his boss' lilting garage, planed it himself
on evenings he was supposed to be working late,
turned each piece with lathe and chisel
until the weave of the tarnished wood
came to life beneath his hands.
He laced the seat from fiber rush cord,
dipping the coils in a pail of warm water
as he went, balancing the moisture and the tension
so the chair could breathe and shift and groan
until it would fit only her hips exactly.

The New Metaphysics

Patricia Gray

Intelligence is a hay rick shining in the sun.
Pitchfork it up and find Bethlehem moldering
and damp, beetles scuttling, and an under-life
that tries to explain things.

Dig deeper. No devil rears, but evil whistles
through you as if you had windows. Religion,
that pearly organism, needs evil. Your body,
a frisky animal, does not always buck away.

Dig now to the center where religion cannot go,
where the closed-captioned self speaks only
when nudged, writing in long, slanted letters,
deciphering the ineffable slowly.

Though the road can be winding and lonely,
stay willing. Risk is a talisman you own.

Twelve

Mark Fitzgerald

Drummers drumming and trees
bearing fruit. The calendar torn apart

for a picture of a waterside hamlet.
December's gondola and Godspeed.
Curses, springs, oxen holding up

the bronze sea. Stars on the crown.
Dreams of gates and precious stones,

the Celestial City. The apostles beside
themselves in the critical moment, how
da Vinci brushed them gesturing

at the rectangular table. Make it round
for King Arthur's knights. Take

a hurricane at top speed and the colors
in the wheel. Face cards. Each step
in recovery. From noon to midnight,

let the jury weigh the decision. Ponder
Virgil's books and Shakespeare's comedy.

Know the cranial nerves, sources
of magnesium, the duodenum. Sleep well
Epiphany eve. Buy a dozen roses, reds

and yellows. Recall the Olympians while
I reach for a photo in black and white:

my father playing basketball, skying
for a rebound at the Palestra in Philadelphia.
His right hand is a foot above the basket,

just touching the ball. He looks so certain,
so determined, young. Captured in mid-air,

my father before he was my father—
Danny and Big Dan, night owl—number 12,
what he wore on his college jersey.

The High Country Remembers Her Heritage

Kirk Judd

My people was music.
Their lives were poems
told in the old language
of earth and season,
rain and sun,
field and sweat,
stream and blood.

My people was music.
They come to this country
in fiddle cases thrown on the tide.
They burst on the shore
and notes was their babies
and they spread over the land,
moving up the valleys and the hollows
with the piping of the wind,
moving up the rivers and the runs
with the rhythm of the spawn,
the pulse of blood on membrane
beating—
coming home to live,
coming home to die,
coming home to live,
coming home.

My people was music.
They throwed down roots
and growed up families and stayed.
Stand with your heart in the earth
and your hand in the sky
and hear 'em in the hum of the planets,
in the songs of the stars
that carry the cadence of time.
Hear your grandaddy in the high fiddle string,
your rogue uncle in the banjo ring,
your button-shoe aunt in the corner guitar

keeping time   keeping time   keeping time.

Hear 'em in there 'cause that's where they is!

My people was music.
They didn't have no politics, nor economics.
They didn't write no newspapers, nor history books.
That's not how their legacy is kept.
Their lives are the poems of my soul,
and the songs of my breath.

My people was music,
and if you wanna know,
you got to be able to *hear* . . .

Mother Revolution

Joshua Gray

The sex was always best at planting time.
The seeds were buried alive in the softened ground,
Where death was found to root among the crops
Of revolution, creeping in the farmer's minds.
Their instruments both looked and felt like weaponry.
Stalking nourishment was torn apart, or ripped from rooted land.
Barefooted, they trampled grapes to make their wine,
And grains were finely crushed with roughened hands.
And thus, the seed of thought sprouted plants of sacred realms.

Human sacrifice replenished farmer's gold, and so
Holistic give-and-take played out in temple caves,
Returning to the source like dying plants when cold wind blows.
The Mother myth reflected famine, drought, and nature's force;
Her consorts were all dismembered, killed before they rose
With the crops of new life. Like men before them, women wandered far
On quests, their deathly struggles restored the harmony and peace
To mother and child from risk of baby's birth,
Seed to womb, seed to earth, the pain of sacred sex at planting time.

Cool Santa Anas

Judy Kronenfeld

Whole days made up of intensities
of light—as if the rays that pierce
clouds in Baroque paintings
were gathered in multiple sheaves
and fanned out melting
into that cloudless profound
blue that beams
I am purity incarnate—

and an excitement,
as if of revelation about to come,
in the basking honeyed warmth
lifted and swept away by currents
of chill, then set down again—

tumbleweeds bounce up
like girls playing hopscotch,
leaf crumble, small twigs, scurry back
on the sidewalk, like water sucked
into the ocean before the next wave.
And then quiet.

And isn't that what
we need—a perfection of contentment edged
by violent change, change edged
by contentment, never to be grounded,
as the body grounds itself to a drug
which then loses its rush, over
and over again to be removed from
and returned to our illusions:
that if only we could stop
doing what we must do now, stop
shunning what we once did, leave home, come
home, burn home, build home,

we would arrive
at happiness.

. . . Leaf litter lull on the lawns, then
cottonwood gold gyring, like wheat
tossed in the air, revealing the sinuous
wind . . .

North Wind, Lunenburg Bound

Trevor Tingle

This grey-green water does not churn,
but we do
as we press our passage against wind and foam,
staggering across deck with time's crooked step
worn into pit and groove.

A pale bath of light marks this morning
like a highlighter on the myth of our lives.
We laugh, bitch, then laugh again
as we thrash
and lash a sail's talkative canvas tongue,

then return astern listening to the legs
of our slickers whisper a slip-slop song.

And still the bilge rises with the sun.

January

Patricia Gray

Cold Moon, Moon of the Terrible,
white ice glistening on snow.
Razors of light rend the surface,
as a hungry howl enters our spines,
touching the lunacy spot. Wine,
dance us glittering in hearthlight;
wind be shut out. Cooking Moon
sing "cauldron simmer." We'll
wassail away cabin fever, parade
our charades, fire-poke and feed
the grate, cornpop and squiggle our feet,
make toasts to each other's moon tongue.
Speaking calumnies together,
we'll summon the Wolf Moon tonight.

Afterglow

Mark Fitzgerald

Summer is ending for miles
on water, departing with the late
sun on the docks, sinking like a whisper

into a green-blue bay. In lingering
light, a small boat bumps against
the pier, reminding me of a song I used

to play over and over. As much as
the lyrics, it was the mood that mattered—
a bare melancholy, a dressed-up nostalgia.

Pacing back and forth in the half-dark,
I heard it differently each time. Summer
was ending then too and I didn't want

to go back to school. Now the same
song glows in the dark brows
of fishermen. In what they caught

and let go. Wordless by the bay,
I savor it in oysters and vinegar.
Summer is ending as a small boat

bumps softly. The mood still matters,
what's made plain in near-darkness,
what shines in a black, cloudless sky.

Butterfly Effect

Joshua Gray

The birth of a butterfly signals another life
lost to metastases. Every elegant monarch
resting on the leaf of a turning maple is the spirit
of a mother, a brother, another friend.

With each flap of its bright wing,
the monarch alters the delicate course
of our lives. Every breath it takes is full
of a departed soul.

A feathered beast can lose its valor.
The eagle is fragile and flees into the forest
whenever it's been forgotten.

But the eagle will always soar into the wind
to carry us along
the frayed path of a butterfly.

Voyager: Petroglyphs at Salt Rock

Kirk Judd

With all the technology and skill they could muster,
they left here, on the rock,
birds, and turtles, and deer,
and a map of the river valley,
and a picture of me.
They sent it hurtling through time to proclaim
"This is who we are
and where we live
and what we have."

Skipping past the last planet's influence,
the spinning craft flashed into the free universe.
It contains recordings of our music and our mathematics,
expressions of our poetry and science,
a map of our solar system
and a picture of me.

Built and launched
with all the technology and skill we could muster,
it screams to the scintillant stars,
"This is who we are
and where we live
and what we have."

"I am here," this poem says.
I sent it to tell you of this time,
of this arrogant yet beautiful species of being.
We are capable of great grace, and great terror,
in touch with timeless wonder
but holding this planet hostage to our social whims
while we slowly realize our relationship with the whole,
our brotherhood with each other
with every shining part, from the bird on the rock
to the laser dance of the spaceship,
each thing born of the blinding bright crack of the void
each thing carried in the common heart of each one,
each thing reminding us,

"This is who we are
and where we live
and what we have."

It is not hard to see myself
someday trying to translate this,
contemplating the me who wrote it,
wondering in subdued awe,
"What was he thinking,
where did he come from,
and where did he go?"

Stargazing on Fire Mountain

John Most

some moments
in real life
say real life
isn't real

by shouting
the fabrications
and the double-
talking patterns
or by turning
into percussive
pigeons or
flooded plains.

it's not that they're
anomalous. it's
not that they
possess an aura
or mystique.

once you've left
behind what can
be sensed, there
are projections.

Out of the Wind You All but Loved

Mattie Quesenberry Smith

Let there be a consolation for sorrows
Whispered from earth to heaven;
Let there be a consolation for explosions,
Dissolutions, dismemberments, severances,
And bloody issues. It is said consolation
Streams from heaven to Earth,
So you grab the hem, knowing
That out of the wind you all but loved
You can expect a miracle: the ship, secured;
Hems, sails, and ropes—all fulfilled by wind.
You can expect it before the wind,
Before it transpires the ocean,
Before it strikes the mast.

Stretch

Sam Brown

Too rapid, too much
Faded, yet noticeably present rivers
Snaking along   the surface
Prance by the riverbed
Where lightning strikes
And scatters scars across the skin
A victorious battleground
For a never-ending war
May fingertips trace each hill
Pinks and reds crescendo on your skin
That artists would envy
We have creams and oils to
Try to hide nature's aftermath
A mirror may whisper that you are not beautiful
It lies

Predawn Eastern Sky

Laura Patterson

There you are half-burnt in the eastern sky
wondering when I'm coming back for you . . .

Your illness   wife blindness
your sickness   the trickster
our lives are your small deaths
flung higher and large
fantasy skylight all navy and pinholes
reality cardboard that puckers and spits
I've seen through this madness   cynic forgiveness
deader than deadness   dove gray complexions
that start to look tender blue under eye circles laughing at fresh
what could new bodies teach us? celestial or other—
we're better off gaping for planets we miss
and how dare your body keep craving and praying
you're dying you're dying and   (why don't you get this?)
the flesh of your own star is all that you own

Editing Poems During a Hospital Deathwatch

Stephen Corey

Dear Poet:

I'm sorry, but I couldn't use your art
today to soothe or distract me from this death—
not quite accomplished yet, but pressing out
as twitchings of her cold and curling feet,
as ulcerous brown blood seeping with her breath.
I expect, had you known, you might have sent
something more attuned to the current path
my mother-in-law is facing. I'm sure
you're thinking this private critique unfair,
and you'd be right to be upset, except
that you'd be wrong. This place, right here, is where
we *always* meet: Beatrice with her chart
devoid of final blessings, you and I
searching for the words that nail sensation to the sky.

Vehicular

Marc Harshman

You come round a curve, the blind crest of a hill
and suddenly there are these two lives waiting
for you, comedic and tragic together, waiting
for you who are to be an instrument from the ancient Greek stage,
you who are to be as innocent as we ever are with chance
and the bad luck of being human.

You see a cobalt-blue Duster jacked up in the near middle of the road.
You see two statues that could be people.
You even see the Holsteins in the distance, the white barns,
the last light of day, the curious moment within which
this new story has to begin.

The seconds divide themselves slowly at first, offering time its
true nature.
The drunk boyfriend, cell to his ear, continues to stand, back to
the action.
The girl straightens her shoulders and then, wide-eyed,
slow-mo, she runs . . .
runs the wrong way on the wrong side
of that wrong road on that wrong day.

The Duster was a solid.
The girl was a blur of time frozen.
The boy was peripheral.
You were driving the company's pickup, a Chevy S10.
You were thinking things through, being careful
and human, being as good
as the unlucky innocent ever can be,
when the seconds began accelerating
and you were dropped into instinct, and swerved
to avoid a collision with that blue Plymouth, swerved
into time, that blur, that little motion, that fleeting last
second of a life, the blood and bone of it, and it was
only a small sort of bump, quiet, and was behind you
as quickly as it had been before you,
behind you where the new seconds began
without any screaming to tick the silence forward

into your own time and place that gathers around you now at night,
alone, without anything so solid as steel and bone,
as even the slender words in the town obituary
that would carry her name, without anything to anchor you
but this moment that refuses to move beyond that glance
back over your shoulder where the living die
without your impatient wish to be perfectly forgiven
even this . . . your almost perfect innocence.

Sexual Violence

Seth Michelson

Watch my teen niece, vegan, snap
the leg off a roasted chicken
and you'll get it: how easily
the body is unmade. It's the carving plate,
to dinner, a hungry family set to feast
on thigh, breast, and wing
of decapitated creature.
Whose mind, the philosopher asked,
is inconsequential in its absence?
Not my niece's, stalked
by thoughts of home invasion:
late at night, alone, in bed half-
dreaming, when she wakes to a window
shattered, footfall nearing her room
where she squints into outer darkness
and sees nothing but her own panted fear,
till he's on her: growling
hot into her ear, his stench
all sweat and sperm and beer,
pinning her at knife-point to her sheet—
how horrifying the eaters' smiles
at the plate of skinned meat, broken bones.

The Pale Goth Fastens Her Dress

Nicole Yurcaba

I wear his safety pin in a secret place:
        below the right breast, four inches,
pinning the place where a button left.

Fastened,
the pin remains safe, secure, disarmed
of piercing the flesh
        that lies beneath.

Unclasped, it bears potential.

Life/Force

Sarah Murphy

It rattles around my feet
and under the pads of my toes,
dignity/grace
rising over my legs
the fiery chasm
between my hefty thighs
cupped in the remnant
of the umbilical
cord
which once
gave life
now bereft
it glows in my belly
filling + stretching
until whitish bolts
razor my skin.
It climbs my spine
clenching handholds of vertebrae
footholds of desire
as it climbs into my heart,
folding itself
into the chambers
and racing through my veins,
all energy
shimmying through my nerves
into my fingertips
grasping my temples
and split ends
until compassion
radiates from my cornea + pupil
pushed through bloodshot sclera
crowning the beam
of everything
through the final eye
that remains
unseen.

The Imaginary Doctors

Judy Kronenfeld

take your hands into their own
raw, rough ones—humbled
by boiling the hospital
linens—red stars bursting
at the nailquicks of nervous
sympathy. They lie down
beside you on the cold tile
floor, by the still waters.
They shepherd your removal
into spacious, newly remodeled
Green Pastures. They take
patient lessons in the lip-sync
of the terminally in terror.

The messages on their machines
sprout wings like the transfigured
hearts in centuries-old emblems
and ascend until the single pyramidical
eye of the doctor blinks them
in.

In the operating theater
they take no bows.

Their silent emissary
bends his young head
as you drive by the window
of the Kwik-View Funeral Parlor.

They bring expensive roses
to the sickroom of your heart,
they come from vast distances,
they pour the milk of space
into pitchers for your bedside table.
And when you are shaking
in the anteroom of the abyss, they,
and not their attendant
choirs, bring warmed blankets

which they tuck around you,
and, like your dead mother,
spit twice, and kiss your forehead.

13 ways of looking at less invasive open heart surgery

It was evening all afternoon. —Wallace Stevens

Barry Gross

I

what's your name?
what's your birth date?
how do you feel?

II

solid young nurses
stretch me taut like a fitted sheet.

III

shaved, nipple to ankle.
i've no choice.
i've given myself over.
i've got nothing but trust.

IV

you have the perfect body
for this operation.
i've never had the perfect body
for anything.

V

knocks, before i respond, walks in.
i shake the last drops
into the plastic urinal
say, just finishing up,
you say, i'll be back.
no shame. no embarrassment.
just necessity and function.

VI

i'm supposed to defecate
but i've too many pain killers.
all there is is flatulence.

VII
ribs spread,
chest artery clipped,
attached to heart,
close up, let it drain.

VIII
half-awake,
baby-bird mouth
pleads for moisture.
ice-chips for aridity,
morphine for off-cliff ache

IX
soft sputters of pain
straighten crooked moments
window of geometric bricks
no obvious passage of light
or shadow or time

X
unpacked from inside chest,
three foot of surgical tubing
to aid in the drain.

XI
i'm the youngster on this floor.
others buried frailties
in fresh linen and IV lines.

XII
tired of waiting for wheelchair.
i walk out door
hugging heart-shaped pillow
propelled by labored half-breaths

XIII
comfort food tastes dull,
breeze dries freshly washed clothes,
monthly bills need to be covered,
8 prescriptions to be consumed.

Symbiote

Joshua Gray

She doesn't give you Herpes.

Instead, she dons
a loosely-fitted spaghetti-strapped red dress,
and begins on your shin. She lowers
to cover the ankle, creeps onto the knee
and anchors herself. It is the only time
her weight is felt.

With increased momentum, she moves in
over the stomach, the chest, the back.
She bruises your neck. As you sleep,
she French kisses your open mouth.

When you wake up, you discover
she's even found the insides
of your elbows. You do not fail to notice
she took some time on your hips.

The only way to free yourself
is to allow your emotions
to possess you.

But she doesn't give you Herpes—
you give it to yourself.

Let's Pretend

William Sypher

My mother died two years ago.
We buried her today,
an unspeakable delay.
She was still breathing
so we waited till she stopped.
Propped her up,
pretended we could talk.
It's the respectful thing to do,
is it not?

We just prolonged her death.
For whom, the bootless breath?
No hope of cure, or even slight reversal,
she just grew worse. This cursed
disease nibbled by degrees
but left her looking normal,
which put us at our ease.

Hospice staff with good intent,
smooth engines of disguising death,
hummed gracefully to the end,
but do the dying want such grace?
Do they like the game of "Let's pretend?"

We are what issues from our minds,
not from parts below it.
Heart to heart is little more
than wistful, mindless metaphor.
No gentler way to put it:
below the brain we do not jibe;
heart-lung machines do not transcribe
sensate conversations.

When our brains have gone so have we.
It's there for all to see, but we reject it
for a rising, falling chest, if we detect it.

Of the living we demand

a modest sensibility.
With the dying we conspire
to show it's not so burdensome
to talk for years with no reply that fits.
We prattle on in daily skits:
loving, congenial lying.

Ten Years

Hiram Larew

What would it have been like
If you had had a brother—
To trust someone like a bottle of dried glue
To never use blankets
To live this life as though you could always see
The ocean just beyond cornfields
Or smell common sense yawning close by

Whatever you'd give to each other you'd probably get back
As pieces of pie
Maybe by leaving each other
You'd get even closer
All you really know is that you will never know
The sky or square that's a brother

Instead try to imagine his spirit
As if he was real—
Not the night so much but an evening
A wheelbarrow left out in the rain
Or some beautiful anger traced around
The shape of a head

Try to live like not a twin exactly
But a kind of double longing
Or think of hair that gets cut too short
But starts all over again
Anyway.

Why We Should Not Brag About Our Emotional Depth

Ed Zahniser

Imagine you're a married woman whose name
does not match the name on your birth certificate
or your passport. You are at the Department of
Motor Vehicles standing in line for so long your idea
of what the initials DMV might mean has changed.
"'Department of Motor Vehicles,' my ass!" Then
you panic, "Did I say that out loud?" because at last
you are nearing the counter and don't yet know
you will be told you lack two more pieces of I.D.
—and, no, your present driver's license is not
acceptable I.D. *What!* To cut to the chase, at that
you may now run through a range of emotions
as complex as a symphony orchestra, which,
incidentally, now plays loud, loud and up-tempo
discordantly inside your head. Could you step back
to observe this panoply of feelings, you might
be tempted to succumb to a fit of species pride,
thinking we're alone in our affective complexity.

Resist: The emotional repertoire of sentient beings
evolved—or was created—in so deep, deep a past
that even worms behave with sophistication,
and baby elephants, on weaning, throw tantrums
worthy of frustrated two-year-old humans.
Male Orca whales have enmeshed relationships
with their mothers that would give Oedipus
a complex. And do not neglect to factor in
that average sperm whale brains outweigh ours
six to one. Or that our mammalian family tree's
taproot was a one-inch-long marsupial
two hundred million years ago that needed
to dodge being stomped flat unseen by dinosaurs.
Admit it: we all resent people whose power
over us is bestowed, not earned. But calm down.
Go back home. Amass enough more I.D. items
to choke that clerk, should you be forced
to jam it down his or her "DMV" gullet.

Heartwood

Steven Knepper

The last stave split and stacked,
The maul and wedges stowed,

Cold slides a long, thin finger
Down his back, provokes a shiver.

He winds the scarf she made
Around his neck and face

While at their home she sets
A rack beside the stove

Where his wet clothes will steam
From cracking heartwood heat

When peeled from legs and chest,
His naked dimpled flesh

Waiting for her to knit
Her unshawled limbs with his,

Their task of keeping warm
Reduced to simplest form.

Refuse

Andrew Manyika

You treated me like garbage
Then decided it was beneath you
To be seen sifting through the trash,
So, you left,
me,
lying in a heap,
lying in the heap,
of refuse
keeping company with all the other unwanted things,
for which the owners could now find no use.

Space-Time

Andrew Manyika

She said,
I need a little space,
I need a little time,
I need a little something,
To clear out my mind

I didn't know she was a physicist,
Or the value she placed on her experiments,
Or that I would be one of the many things she'd leave behind,
While searching for herself in the quilt-work fabric
Of Space and Time.

Time

Heather Banks

If I ask, will you tell me
the time now
how much time is there
where does it go
the time that was
time together
time to go?

What is the difference
any way, some how
between one time
some time, any time
first times, good times
hard times, last times?

With continents apart
and no firm place
to stand on
does time stop, stand still
and what about the flying time?

Is time the mass of energy
squared in the speed of light?

How can we tell
what time is
relevant
to each other
to us
to our selves?

I do not know yet how much we have
but there is this time
to be.

Trying on clothes

Sophy Burnham

When you come to think about it,
It's stories we're trying on
All the time and taking off
Like clothes in the closet or Macy's dressing room.
We plunk down dollars for the daily news
Or tune to tales on Fox or NPR,
And those are true events, or as true as stories get
When they have to have sewn seams,
Frills and finished hem.
When we grow bored
We read a novel or biography
Or else indulge in gossip,
Which is another word for tattletales
About our friends or enemies; and finally
We tug over our heads sometimes
The tales we tell ourselves,
The sweater of *I'm Not Enough,*
Which looks pretty good on you, I'd say,
Then reconsider, no,
Not Good Enough, and change it for the
Turtleneck of *Downright Failure, Never*
Amount to a Hill of Beans,
Told You So,
Fake, fraud, passé.

You twirl before the mirror, head cocked,
Assessing how the skirt swishes
Sexy at the knee, considering how
This one's pretty good except
I'm A Victim hangs on a hook nearby
All pleats and ruffles, tempting, and
Here's a winter coat untried so far, so
On with that one too: *Too Late, Too Old, Washed up.*
It's sorta okay, but you want to
Go back to the turtleneck

That felt so warm and comfy, an old friend:
Failure, Hill of Beans, Told you So, You Fake:
That's a story I can get real mileage from.

My warm clothes

Sharif Al-Shafiey
translated by Amr El-Zawawy

My warm clothes
With the whiff of the first summer breeze,
I moved my warm clothes to the remotest point in my wardrobe,
Turning a deaf ear to the meteorologists' warnings
About weather changes.

I rearranged the whole wardrobe.
I gazed at my military suit for a long time,
Not knowing where to put it indeed.
Shall I get rid of it?
I do not think I will get a formal summons.
"We are not in a state of war,"
At least as morning newspapers
And news briefs say.

Strangely, I selected the best hook
And hung the military suit on
In the nearest point in the wardrobe,
Only to sleep soundly,
Certain that no one will dare steal my wife's jewelry
From the upper shelf.

When I slept afterwards,
I dreamt of running in the scorching sun,
Clad in a helmet and military boots only,
Carrying a machine gun.

I tried to kill stray dogs,
Which forced my wife to collect her sheep
And to leave her wooden cottage on the mountain.
I fired the bullets in vain.
All dogs melted in fortresses and troughs.

I woke up tired.
I found the thieves had completely destroyed the wardrobe.
The jewelry was intact. . . . Thank God!
Yet sons of a bitch had stolen my military suit.
Did they covet the hook?!

The Mosque that Built Itself

William Sypher

In Adam, hard scrabble center of Oman,
tales of a self-made mosque live on.
Scions of the al-Marooqi clan
talk earnestly of their ancestors
once keen to build a tiny mosque
in an undistinguished spot,
amid some groves of date palms
they passed each morning
on their way to work the fields.

They met one weekday morn
a hundred years ago
when field work was put aside
for this, a grand occasion.
They dug a trench, four meters on a side
gathered stones, mixed mud and straw
and started several rows of bricks.

No one is sure what happened next
but they fell out on the design,
quarreled on thickness of the walls,
perhaps, or where
the tiny windows should be placed.
All we know is that they squabbled,
gave up the job and went their own ways,
blaming each other for the fizzled plan.

Next morning on the way to work,
as they approached the bare, rude spot
where they had left the stunted walls
a foot or so above the ground,
they were struck dumb:
the mosque was full in place.

It had happened overnight in utter
desert darkness. No one near
had seen light from torches
that could have lit the ghostly build.

Too much for mortal men to grasp,
no matter how electrified by faith.

It must have been Allah. Yes, that was it.
These men were primed to credit miracles,
but guilt crept in and doubt came after.
Why would Allah reward
those who had clashed
then sulked and slunk away
from a holy project
on newly hallowed ground?
What lesson could that teach?
Was he shaming them?

The mosque now sits abandoned
next to a chugging, oily water pump
that steals from its sacredness.
The story of this self-built mosque
has passed down from man to man,
in the al-Marooqi clan,
still tinged with guilt,
still scratching their heads.

Coffee Break

Maryann Wolfe

I am fed in half-sandwich increments:
a half of his sandwich
when I happen to walk in the kitchen
and find him grilling one.

He asks me to make him coffee—
an indirect request like
"I'm craving coffee" or
"You only drink coffee at night?"

But I know the signal, the pre-measured
dose, and how to use the commercial
coffee maker so not a drop of water
hits the floor.

Two spoons, two mugs, a little milk,
for me, the bag of Holly brand sugar.
What does it mean? Another slow
day at work, us lingering over coffee
while another sandwich grills for us to split.

In the store, the fan whirrs its Monday circle
and soon the delivery people will arrive,
but for now, it's half a sandwich and another
piece of his story—David hasn't called
for his new schedule.

And I will share another piece of mine—
her boyfriend is in jail and this morning
her husband and oh, wait, let me
grab the phone because that story
is a whole sandwich long.

Ode to Bacon

Andrew Manyika

Bacon,
We never knew you
Yours is the sweet savour of a Saturday morning,
Scintillating scent transcending space, and perhaps time,
Titillating taste teasing tongue and perhaps mind,
Placed on plates while I cleared the palate,
Among taste-buds you had pride of place, my mouth—your palace

Bacon!

You, who moved from forbidden fruit, to breakfast staple
Oh, the hopeless emptiness when you are absent from the breakfast table,
Devoured in a flurry of gobbledygook,
We chewed and munched and gobbled now look,
All that remains,
Is a plate marked with grease stains,
And the unspoken question lingering in our brains,

"does it really come from a pig's rear end?"
Oh, my dear dear friend,

Bacon,
we never knew you
(and perhaps that was for the best)

Pomegranate

Laura Patterson

witches' tools in wooden bins
stiffly   forgiving
each fingerprint dent
a whisper—*Change*

What is it, Mommy?
Put that back. We don't need it.

who am I to digest the indigestible?

the negative of a baseball glove
weighty and mad
red leather   once burnished
abandoned to rain

penance requires research
Joy of Cooking:
In the water, the light rind
and pith will float
and the heavy seeds sink.

scored and tattered   an interior skin
organ casing honeycombed to rubies
red delight   scarlet disgust
spiraling inward
familiar as bone

The Pale Goth Buys Blank Journals at Target

Nicole Yurcaba

Mommy, is that a Halloween decoration?
No, it's just someone who's . . . very different.

A Volvo-driving soccer mom and her pigtailed little girl move to the
next aisle
after spotting me perusing stationery. The mother's probably putting
Play-Doh in the cart and telling her daughter *Don't you ever*
come home dressed like that!

I pluck a college-ruled journal from the cream-colored metal shelf.
On the cover, green owls and purple foxes play together beneath
a pink and blue tree. The little girl would declare the owls and foxes
"cute" and "adorable."

Her mother would remind her *Remember, honey, owls aren't purple,*
and foxes aren't green, and trees aren't pink and blue, but
when you mix pink and blue you might get purple, but it won't be
an owl because owls aren't purple, and don't dress in all black
because the knight in shining armor won't love you if you
dress in black and own a black cat named Nosferatu and…

I leave the stationery aisle, journal in hand, imagining
the verses and words, the dreams, that will flood its lines;
I pass the aisle
where the little girl and her mother stand, and as I pass
the little girl turns, and she waves, shyly, so her mother
won't notice as she's choosing what shade
of white Play-Doh to place in the cart.

A Very Tall Building

for Anacreon
John Most

there's a haze that loves
surprise. its structures
reflect then light up.
nothing is more unbound
than a shocked mind. your
mind, a terrain changing

like the Harding Icefield,
shuts out, shuts in—let
it be.   the sunlit
city is a world—a
pack of thoughts—and its

people throw dance
at the beats of urges

anything can start it

nothing can stop it

falling into you,
the vision breaks apart

Icarus's Choice

Sam Brown

My favorite story is that of Icarus
The story of a boy whose ambition was his demise
People always remember that he soared too high
But forget that he was warned not to dive too low
Many things in life get forgotten
Like how curiosity killed the cat
But satisfaction brought it back
Or that blood is thicker than water
When it's the blood of the covenant
That's thicker than the water of the womb
People are told to follow their dreams
And to not aim too low
But are criticized for pursuing what they want
I see a little bit of Icarus in all of us
Bright-eyed, looking for a better future
I believe my family prayed
for me to be anything but a starving artist
A chorus of "Please God, anything but an artist"
They forget that art is a staple of our world
That without artists, the world would be dull
I like to believe that Icarus had a pleasant view
Right before he drowned
Before the waves crashed over him
I'm sure he had a lover
Or a dream
Or just a reason to live
Could he tell which way was up or down
When the waves overtook him?
Did he flail and fight to live?
Or did he accept his fall from grace?

Fishing from the Roof of the House

Jen Karetnick

This is no Hemingway tale.
The fish we catch are not fabled
and will not make our fortune,
harnessed to nothing more
than some jerk spices
and the bottom of a frying pan
liberally coated with oil
so the flesh will not stick
as ours does to the sheets
we lie on at night
when the waves have quieted
like overtired children. We cast
sidearm the way we used to
heave a baseball into mitts
to avoid throwing the brims
of each other's hats
into the ocean with the bait,
although this has happened,
and this is what we have reeled in:
saturated reminders of another life
when the mean seats of a marlin
stadium meant a blistered nose
for a couple of days and not this
flooded, floorless amphitheater
where the only entertainment
is skin after peeling skin,
eternal, infinite, varying only
in hit, fight and run.

Impressions

Dawn Leas

In a bright blue bowl, she mixes
cement from purple to pink
explains the process
through a paper mask,
glasses poised on tip of her nose.
She fills a tray and holds
it against my top teeth
waiting for it to set white.

Brushing pieces of hardening
cement from my chin, she says
she reads poetry at night.

Neruda in Spanish
Rilke in German
takes notes on translations—
cadence changes, nuances,
untranslatable phrases.

She tugs on metal tray to release
its bond, grabs another bowl
and begins mixing again—

if you don't know who Langston Hughes is, she says, you've
never read poetry.

Guinivere's Apple

Stan Galloway

"Tristram's dead," was all he said, and took
my hand to show his sympathy. Our eyes
turned down, unmet, and studied there a bowl
of apples freshly laid by morning's maid.

His fingers slid across my hand, unbidden,
warm, and dandled at my cuff, as if
to say, "We should have guessed," "We tried our best,"
or "Nothing more that you or I can do."

This was the hand that in the night had soothed
the daylight tensions, offered grace, accepted
me, assured my place beside him on
the throne, still warm and strong upon my own.

The apples glinted lively in the sun.
They, too, suggested warmth and firmness meant
to comfort, their bright redness overcoming
dull clay tinted gray from sturdy use.

I heard him sigh, a signal that our thoughts
for him must be respectful and regretful.
Nothing less would fit our station, nothing
else express a measured, fit goodbye.

My thoughts rode back two fortnights hence to weigh
some sense from Tristram's parting words with me.
"I cannot stay," he said. "My heart is gone
and I must go to it." He was resolved.

"But hearts," I said, "and wills are not the same.
Each part builds something larger—whole." He sneered and
lifted both hands to the moonless sky
and sifted air: "No heart—no life worth having."

He'd return, I thought. He'd gone before,
so many times, to Brittany and Cornwall,
Lyonesse and Ireland; he *would*
return with songs and rhymes, I thought. Farewell.

"How did it happen?" were the words I heard
come from my lips. The words were hardly mine
but there was no one else to speak them. Slowly
Arthur raised his head, spurred by my voice.

My furtive eyes, with tact, observed him fix
the stone with meek command, to speak the message.
"Bedivere has said that he was taken
in the act of wooing Cornwall's queen."

This practiced proclamation from his royal
voice showed me his loyal, distant stance.
He would take time to reconcile words
with fateful chance and cold reality.

My Arthur sometimes lagged in joining thought
and act, deliberate to grasp the impact
of the words on life. He dragged his eyes
with self-control to view the bowl of apples.

Red and bold they sat, plucked yesterday,
engendered by the tree that whispered through
the window, latent energy abiding,
each one waiting for its time to come.

His finger traced a line along my own
then he looked up, returned, his smile crooked
as it had been that first time he faced me
in my father's hall when I was nine.

Even then I saw someone that I could
tease with and could trust. He'd pulled the sword
in London just that day it seemed. His famous
reign began for me with that quaint smile.

I wonder where the decades now have gone.
He thirty-eight, I twenty-nine, it seemed
that all our life lay now behind us. News of
death can make the fullest life deflate.

"He was more bold than wise, more heart than brain."
This voice was just for me, his intimate,
his closed-door voice. This voice had told a daughter
in her father's hearing she'd be queen.

Leodogrance had stammered when the king
then asked permission—how the memory makes me
smile—he had given half his castle
in the riant clamor of assent.

I, too, was pleased, though no one asked, to play
my part, unseen, but quite content, as Arthur's
wife and Britain's queen. My role in life
could certainly oblige a lesser station.

"Sure, he was," the voice went on, "a man
addicted to amusement." *Female charm*,
he meant. "He never quite grew up, and yet
the best knight of the tournament hands down.

"Life was ever just a game to do.
His friends were pawns and knights and rooks, no bishops;
he did ever aim to check the queen—
not you, of course, but figuratively."

He chuffled at the metaphor he made.
"And now the black king's castled at the cost
of his dear queen." "Isolt?" I asked, alarmed.
"Dying from the blade that pierced *his* back.

Unwise, like Zimri with some princess-whore
from Midian, he pushed incautiously
right through her chamber door. King Mark then coldly
entered to dispatch them with one thrust."

I winced to think this privacy now shouted
from the castle roofs. I was convinced
such shame occurred for hadn't Gawen and
Ettard done quite the same though lived to tell?

But Tristram was no goat like Gawen, nor
was he an Absalom to use such means
to claim a throne. No, Tristram's silver throat
was champion of song and game and joust.

He was the darling of the court. His tongue
delighted lord and maid alike. He'd sung
to king and peasant, challenged noblemen
on board or field. His only foe was envy.

Who would not have gladly changed his place,
his name, his face, with Tristram? Who would spurn
the chance to please so many? Every woman's
head would turn to find that voice's face.

He'd flattered me, I've never told, when I
first came to Camelot. "The dragon's fire
never flares too close to his own heart,"
he said as spry insurance from the flame.

I hadn't thought of Arthur as a dragon.
Hand on mine, his gentleness swam over
other faults. One hardly noticed when he
sought more than he gave or snubbed a slave.

I'd swept aside the proposition deftly
as a courtesy, a compliment
acknowledged but rejected. So he sighed
and slept with someone else to soothe his hurt.

I didn't know him then as I do now.
Perhaps I never really knew him as
I could have, as I should have. His a heart
on show was much more obvious than mine.

Yet, what a heart! I envied his audacious
risk, his verbal art, his *jeu d'esprit*
that rivaled even Dinadin. When he
called Arthur "king of doormats" how I'd glared.

But two months later every straggling knight
could wield a lance much better than before,
each sword could bite much sharper, every rebel
lord began to yield to Arthur's name.

This Arthur benefited, won renown
because a forest knight had dared affront
the crown. No grasper, he was gone when Merlin
bared the Table seats folk talk about.

That crown lay cold on Arthur's head, with more
than one great benefactor dead, gone down
in battle or in shame. And like his smile,
tilted, honor sat in hints of gray.

"You're quiet, Mead," he said. I smiled weakly,
here amiss, looked down. A pet name, Mead,
I hated it yet never told him so;
he said my honey kisses made him drunk.

So I became his mead while others used
a cup. He meant to be endearing, I
concede, but failed in this attempt. "My wit
is bruised," I said. "Forgive me. I'm distracted."

"Understandable." His hand moved to
the apple bowl and traced the Roman figures
crudely inked in former times. Their days
had faded, lost like hour-glass sand displaced.

Respectful of my silence, patient-flawed,
he sat. Where lay the vigor that had burned
to rally men in tournament and battle?
Tristram was not so. I turned away.

The window framed a glorious day. Along
the road a knight in blue and silver trappings
rode a gray horse to the apple tree.
He took the aimed-down lance and raised it up.

He snaked it firmly up between the brown
and green to reach a well-protected apple
left alone upon the crowning branch,
aspiring tip stretched high as it could go.

He shook the branch to make the ready apple
fall. Then leaning out he dropped the lance,
and tumbling from the horse, he caught the tumbling
apple, pulled it to him, took the fall.

He bruised himself but not the tender fruit
he'd so retrieved. He got up from the dust.
He took the treasure to his lips and tasted
full the sweetness he believed he'd find.

I thought that I could taste his triumph, taste
the salty sweetness on my tongue, my nose
could smell the soft bouquet, my eye could see
delicious satisfaction swell within.

I pulled the bed of apples to me, just
outside the reach of Britain's king and took
the topmost apple, red, imploring, to my
teeth and bit into the white-dark core.

Just Work On

Ed Zahniser

Renoir tied the paintbrush
to his hand and painted on
through the arthritic pain
and Bob Dylan
with arthritis still touring
playing not much guitar
but keyboards now
whereas
Mickey Mantle switch-hit
until his knees gave out
then switched to booze like
something had been lost

The trick is in the knowing
nothing's lost—
you find the hand wrap
switch from guitar to keyboards
watch to see where your breath
turns in the tube to
your portable oxygen tank
and how the light glints off
that point like off ancient
Egyptian icons revealed
in Giacometti's skinny
sculptures

Just work on

Who's That with the Horn

John McKenna

"Hey, who's that? Who's that cat with the horn?"

"Who is that, you ask . . .
who's kinda blue in kinda royal purple? Huh?
huh, who, on the corner—right there right now right close
not but a blink away
like the sky so wide open
ever expanding expansive standing commanding

Who? Who is that studying it all, man?
standing head up
and down
Beat up
beat down
beat-to-beat
beat-iful!!!!

Smiling anywhere everywhere behind that
the good silver cup chalice
poured shared and sure—yeah!

Who the hell is that zip-krak-cat
all lit up and in the middle of it all
—the center of it all
—how now and it and all
takin' tokin' snakin' smokin'
givin' gettin' lookin' leerin' leanin'
and lift leavin' the scene
and the ground
without even moving his feet

Who, in that just right night tight silent way
in person
in tune
instrumental
insatiable
indescribable
instantaneous

and Immortal
close and closer still yet
the outreaching magnificence
Oracle and Seer
Shaman and Sage
Martyr and Mystic
Music-man and Muse
On wind and black hawk wing

That man, that man there, must have listened to everything—
body and note;
heard everything—body and note
needed to follow no one—chose to findfollowfind the beat the
good beat the new beat
THE BEAT

He is it—Kat Crème Brûlée"
Rip Tip of the Tip Top Pop Top

Slow out!
Gone man gone!!

in some smoke blue in milk with silver streamers
ascended surrender bow when he slowly lowered his head over
his horn
like Buddha in cheshire grin jazz club corner trio
come up and eyes wild new bright radiant

He was in the horn now and the horn was in him
and the beat, THE BEAT had them both
the beat was playing through his blood bones lungs lips fingers
in uninterrupted lines
with that silver wand magic wind machine

White
Black
Silver
Blue
Mace
Magik

That, who is that? Who is that cat with the horn? Who is that?

That baby, that baby is Miles, baby—Miles.

That young'un is Mr. Miles Davis

Miles 'muthafuckin' Davis

Pied Piper of the night delight

Be careful now—He knows All about it. . . .

A Peter Murphy Kind of Night

Nicole Yurcaba

the dream's corridor
   beige   tan
      black-walled
a   man
      finds me
behind glass   fluorescent light
      puckering
strange   fondness
   What happened?
my eyes battered birds
 struggling upward
from terror's ground
   devotion when he
takes me into his palm
his blue opulence
 the   rapture
   Revelations promised

A Poem Written as Scars

Sara Robinson

I read this book about a young woman
who cuts. She carves words into her skin.
It started when she was young and with
each strike she felt relief, though fleeting.

A typewriter key lays ink on the paper
from a ribbon that is struck by the key,
all painless and nice—it leaves its mark:
      Flat, black, and semi-permanent.

But if you cut words into skin
scars will rise once the bleeding
has stopped leaving risen script
etched on a fleshy tableau.

I cannot imagine cutting words into
my skin as much as I love to write
poetry. I find many words I want
to keep for eternity and while my

skin would be interesting for
this preservation I am too afraid
of pain. I could use a Bic and
put the words in ink where I could

see them. That is a good compromise
I think. There is no pain to a
ballpoint "tat" but there has to be some
suffering in the words for them

to tell a story about healing and
the aftermath of scarring one's
body. To feel life or to defer death.
My trembling hand, a trembling pen.

Poems of This Size

Stephen Corey

In poems of this size, so little
might happen, one wonders if such brevity
can matter—as when I strolled, thirty years ago,
with my wife (a year before she *was* my wife)
in her first neighborhood, and we heard
that familiar, horrible squealing of tires down the block.
And because she was a young nurse, no doctor
in sight, when we reached the small boy
lying on the red-brick street with many people
gathered around, she had to step forward and kneel,
had to be the one cradling him and wondering,
most closely, at how quick and full an end can be.

a river of color

Kirk Judd

there is one red apple in the tree.
it is the shade of the feeder on the porch,
the sweatshirt you're wearing.
hummingbirds helicopter out of the forsythia,
rise and hover in front of the fruit,
sway and dart,
dip and chase,
move to the feeder,
to you on the swing.

gnats float on the moist current,
move up and down
in rhythm with our blood,
the pulse in our fingers
passes through the skin
as the gnats pass each other,
bobbing in the blue morning
over the verdant fencerow
where last night the air hung white
above the dodder's pale lace,
waiting for the sky to lose the light
and darken to the color of earth and us.

after dark,
glowworms glittered green,
winked thin laugh lines
under the peavine and ivy,
under the porch steps,
under our eyes.

now, fragrance from some yellow-leafed limb
vibrates a crack in time,
hums memory in my glistening vision,
recalls the smell of split wood,
orange oak flesh from a past visit
when i needed warmth
and took the tree's gift twice,
once in the cutting,

again in the stove.

you push poems from the page,
lush lines temper our senses
the way the wood healed the silver chill.
we cast word spells on each other
throw them around this singing space,
you by reading, me by listening,
both by knowing the poetry
of this moment in our breath,
in the scent of our skin,
in the spark of our eyes.

everything shudders.

the swing pulls the earth
around the sun.
the porch frames the circle
of the wheeling sky.
the fence holds the seed
of every wet, green
growing thing.
the rain shines substance
into the timid wind.
the tree offers the apple
to the sparkling day.

i look at you.
birds laugh their songs,
and god is a river of color
in the shimmering air.

The First Great Beast

John Berry

God

Digging the clouds being foaled
By her fresh yellow sun
And baby-blue ocean

Lies on her back
In her green young fields,
Inspired by shapes, wobbling

Out of her heavens.

Hears the lowing and mewling,
The bellow and roar,
The thrum of the wings,
The squeak and the grunt,

The sonorous songs in the flash
            of the waters
The songs of the night
strummed
            on the lyres of legs

Invents poetry
Under a cloud becoming
The first great beast.

The World's Largest Poet Visits Rural Idaho

Stephen Corey

His 300 pounds on his 6-11 frame
will not fit into the dean's VW
waiting at the bus station. He must wait again
while a forty-mile round trip brings another car.

At the Pine Tree Motel the world's largest poet
piles baggage on the underlength bed,
naps on blankets on the tile floor.

That evening, a low table his only podium,
he ducks and squints to read his poems.

Both he and his hosts are aware of all this.
They have him for the glaciers and wild birds
that spring from his giant fingers.
He's there because the battered humming
in his head will not stop.

Writing Poetry with Putin

Sara Robinson

This time of year the black flies are a distraction.
They emerge from the forest floor, are
restless, and don't appreciate their evolutionary
history. Better to find a mossier spot, perhaps
with better views of the valleys and more
open vistas beyond mountains to the sea.

The wind coming in from the west doesn't
give us the sweetness we thought we
deserved so by moving our blanket to the
slope side facing Balaklava we might catch
a friendlier, warmer breeze, one whose

promise of fertility and longevity offer
up perfect stanzas for our anticipated
listeners. We can create words of love,
inspiration, dedication, wealth, and
even a call to arms in the name of our

muses which we know are found in
the folklore museums of Kiev and Kharkov.
We can take our words, partition them over
and over again until we have the right emphasis
and reverence to proper metrical positions.

We can write in the best style of our homeland
giving into reminiscence of white, stout houses
along winding rivulets of waters which feed
our cows, our wheat, our children, and our
beets. Astride our horses, with our chests bare,

panting, we feel evening turn from warmness
to proudest of dusks into tantamount
cold arrival of darkness. We don't need our coats.
We liberate our own heat from the satisfaction
that we have done all this, our best writing,
our proudest poetry, for the heavy-nailed boot.

Contributors

Sharif Al-Shafiey was born in 1972 at Menouf in Lower Egypt. He received his B.A. in journalism from Cairo University, 1994. He is currently a journalist on the staff of *Al-Ahram Newspaper*. He is the author of five books, including *The Complete Collection of a Robot* (2012). His work has been translated from Arabic into English, French, Italian, and Spanish. "My Warm Clothes" appears here for the first time, translated by Amr El-Zawawy.

Patsy Asuncion, of Charlottesville, Virginia, published, *Cut on the Bias*, (Laughing Fire Press, 2016), her debut collection about the world from the slant of a bi-racial child raised by an immigrant father and WWII vet. Other publications include: Indiana University's *Spirit*, the *New York Times*, *vox poetica*, *Prevention Magazine*, *Snapdragon*, Loyola's *The Truth About the Fact*, *Reckless Writing*, *Armadillo*. The only local female emcee, Patsy promotes diversity through: her open mic (7,000+ YouTube views), local initiatives like Nasty Women Poets and Women of Color as well as community arts as board member of WriterHouse and The Bridge PAL "Back Talk," "Math for Girls Counts," and "Jungle Gym" were previously published in *Cut on the Bias*.

Heather Banks lives in Harrisonburg, Virginia. Born in Nebraska, she lived near Boston for 10 years and in the Maryland/DC area for 40 years. She taught in Taiwan for 2 years, then at the University of Maryland, Montgomery College, and Howard University. She was a writer/editor at the Smithsonian, NIH, a scientific society, and several nonprofits and contractors. Heather has read at numerous venues in Maryland, Pennsylvania, and DC. Her poems have appeared in several literary magazines and two DC anthologies. Her chapbook *Still Life Without Pomegranate* (Eyrie Heath, 2008) was followed by *Split Rail Fence* (Eyrie Heath, 2014). "Time" first appeared in *Still Life Without Pomegranate*; "Only in America" and "Clouds as Links and Diviners" appear here for the first time.

John Berry's first book of poems, *Wobbly Man*, was published in the Spring of 2016. A self-taught woodworker, carpentry contractor and promoter of all things poetry, he writes and works from Winchester, Virginia. John hosts the Shenandoah Poetry Alliance Open Mic at the Handley Library in Winchester Virginia, and an internet TV show entitled The Sock Drawer Poetry Series which airs on WinLifeTV.com.

"The First Great Beast," "West Bound Flowers," and "Brown Rabbit" appear here for the first time.

Dr. **Nadia Boudidah Falfoul** is Assistant Professor at the Faculty of Letters and Human Sciences in Kairouan, Tunisia. She holds a PhD on the discourse of humor in the fiction of contemporary American women writers. Her articles are published in Tunisia, Germany (*Lambert Academic Publishing*), and USA (*Women's Review of Books*). Her major interests: women's feminist writings, contemporary American fiction, modern and postmodern poetry. Her Arabic translation of Stan Galloway's poem "To Sleep" appears here for the first time.

Caroline Brae lives in the mountains of Central Virginia. A former high school teacher of 25 years, she embraced the challenges of students with emotional and learning disabilities. Caroline has since ventured on a creative and artistic 10-year odyssey in the performing arts as a choreographer, dancer, singer/songwriter, and pianist. *Little Grey Bird* is her first poetic endeavor in a long journey to find her voice. Currently, Caroline enjoys pairing her original photography and poetry on Instagram. Her poem "Convergence" appeared originally in *Little Grey Bird.*

Sam Brown, a native of Grottoes, Virginia, is pursuing a degree in English at Bridgewater College. She intends to continue writing poetry while also working on a novel. Her poems "Stretch" and "Icarus's Choice" appear here for the first time.

Best-selling author of 15 books, **Sophy Burnham** has produced award-winning novels and nonfiction, plays, journalism, essays, children's books and short stories. She is most celebrated for writing on angels, mysticism, and the spiritual. Her works are translated into 26 languages. She gives workshops around the country and abroad. Her most recent novel is *Love, Alba* (River Sanctuary Press, 2015); and her poetry, *Falling: Love-Struck, the God Poems* (Finishing Line Press, 2016) where "me stupid," "Words, Words," and "Trying on Clothes" originally appeared.

Stephen Corey published his first poems in the mid-1970s and has worked at the *Georgia Review* since 1983. He has nine poetry collections and recently published his first prose collection, *Startled at the Big Sound: Essays Personal, Literary, and Cultural* (Mercer University Press, 2017). "Editing Poems During a Hospital Deathwatch" and "Poems of This Size" were originally published in *There Is No Finished World* (White Pine Press, 2003); "The World's Largest Poet Visits Rural Idaho" first appeared in *The Last Magician* (Water Mark Press, 1981; reissued by Swallow's Tale Press/ Livingston Press, 1987).

Dr. **Linda Dove** was formerly a professor in international development at the University of London, UK, and later a World Bank official privileged to visit more than 100 countries over 20 years. In her new life as a poet in Virginia's central Shenandoah Valley, Linda reflects on our the world with social comment, spiritual meditation, and satirical humor. Her recent poems have appeared in the *Virginia Literary Journal* and several editions of *The Echo World*. She founded a local poets' group which meets monthly to share and experiment with form and oral presentation. "A Night of Anapests" and "A Late Offer: In Decima" appear here for the first time.

Mahan Ellison is Assistant Professor of World Languages and Cultures at Bridgewater College. "A Dormir," his translation of Stan Galloway's "To Sleep," appears here for the first time. His original poetry has appeared in *The This Magazine*, *Dirty Chai Lit Mag*, and *Black Heart Magazine*.

Mark Fitzgerald is the author of *By Way of Dust and Rain* (Cinnamon Press, 2010) and *Downburst*, which will be published in 2018. His poetry has appeared in many periodicals, including *San Pedro River Review*, *Slipstream*, *Santa Clara Review*, and *Beltway Poetry Quarterly*. His work also appears in *Scratching Against the Fabric* (unbound CONTENT, 2015). Mark teaches writing at the University of Maryland and was recently awarded a writing fellowship from the Virginia Center for the Creative Arts. "Afterglow" was first published in *Slipstream*. "Tiger Lilies" and "Twelve" appear here for the first time.

Stan Galloway, founder and host of the Bridgewater International Poetry Festival, has written 3 chapbooks and one full collection of poetry, *Just Married* (unbound CONTENT, 2013). He is Professor of English at Bridgewater College. "To Sleep" and "Guinivere's Apple" appear here for the first time.

In addition to a verse adaptation of *Beowulf* for young readers, **Joshua Gray** is the author of four poetry collections, most recently *Steel Cut Oats* and *Symposium* (Red Dashboard, 2015 and 2016).

Raised in Northern Virginia, he spent 2012-13 living in India and has since relocated to Tennessee. "Symbiote" was originally published in *Z-Composition* and most recently in *Symposium*, "Butterfly Effect" in *Symposium*, and "Mother Revolution" in *Steel Cut Oats*.

Patricia Gray's poems appeared most recently in *Salamander*, *The MacGuffin* and *Mantis*—and in the 2017 *Tiger's Eye*, accompanied by an interview. A 2016 recipient of the artist fellowship from the DC Commission on the Arts and Humanities, Gray is an alumna of Bread Loaf Writer's Conference. She formerly directed the Library of Congress poetry office and serves on the poetry board of the Folger Shakespeare Library. Fall 2017, she will teach at The Hill Center campus of the Bethesda, Maryland Writer's Center. "The New Metaphysics" was first published in *Salamander*, "Bee Weight" in *The Louisville Review*, and "January" in *Mantis: A Journal of Poetry, Criticism and Translation*.

Barry Gross, of Levittown, Pennsylvania, doesn't remember exactly when he first wrote "Observe and Record" in one of his journals, but he uses that phrase to remind himself why he writes. He's worked as a department store Santa Claus, a stadium beer vendor, window washer, bartender, waiter, cook, proofreader, and teacher. His work has been published in such places as *The Mill Hunk Herald*, *The North Colorado Review*, and *Clarify*. His first book of poetry is *Coiled Logic* (Red Dashboard, 2015). He was a 2016 finalist in the Bucks County Laureate competition. "Thirteen Ways," and "Thoughts Before They Poke a Hole in My Chest" appear here for the first time.

Marc Harshman's latest poetry collection, *Believe What You Can* (West Virginia University, 2016), is the winner of the 2017 Weatherford Award from the Appalachian Studies Association. His fourteenth children's book, *Fallingwater*, co-authored with Anna Smucker, is forthcoming from Roaring Brook/Macmillan. His poems have been anthologized by Kent State University, the University of Iowa, University of Georgia, and the University of Arizona. His other children's books include *The Storm*, a Smithsonian Notable Book. He was an invited reader at the 2016 Greenwich Book Festival in London. His monthly show for West Virginia Public Radio, "*The Poetry Break*," began airing in January 2016. He is the seventh poet laureate of West Virginia. "Vehicular," "Fucked," and "Grandmother at the Dressmakers'" all appeared previously in *Believe What You Can*.

Julie Hensley was raised in the Shenandoah Valley. She traveled west, earning an MFA at Arizona State University. Now she is a core faculty member of the Bluegrass Writers Studio, the low-residency MFA program at Eastern Kentucky University. Hensley is the author of two books: *Viable* (Five Oaks Press, 2015) and *Landfall: A Ring of Stories* (Ohio State University Press. 2016). "Ambrosia" and "Tell Them You Had a Mole Removed" were both originally published in *The Southern Review.*

John Hoppenthaler is Professor of English/Creative Writing at East Carolina University. He is the author of three poetry collections published by Carnegie Mellon University Press, most recently *Anticipate the Coming Reservoir* (2008) and *Domestic Garden* (2015). He also edited, with Kazim Ali, the critical work *Jean Valentine: This-World Company*. "Ice Jesus" was previously published in *Anticipate the Coming Reservoir*.

Kirk Judd, Morgantown, West Virginia, has lived, worked, trout fished and wandered around in West Virginia all of his life. Kirk was a member of the Appalachian Literary League, a founding member and former president of West Virginia Writers, Inc., and is a founding member of and creative writing instructor for Allegheny Echoes, Inc. Author of three collections of poetry including *My People Was Music* (Mountain State Press, 2014), and a co-editor of the widely acclaimed anthology *Wild, Sweet Notes—50 Years of West Virginia Poetry 1950–1999*, he is widely published. "Voyager," "a river of color," and "The High Country Remembers Her Heritage" were all previously printed in *My People Was Music*.

Jen Karetnick is the Miami-based author of seven collections of poetry, including *American Sentencing* (Winter Goose Publishing, 2016), which was a long-list finalist for the Julie Suk Award from Jacar Press, and *The Treasures That Prevail* (Whitepoint Press, 2016), a finalist for the 2017 Poetry Society of Virginia Book Award. Her work has appeared recently or is forthcoming in *The Evansville Review*, *Negative Capability*, *One*, *Prime Number Magazine*, *Spillway*, *Verse Daily* and *Waxwing*. She works as the Creative Writing Director at Miami Arts Charter School as well as a dining critic, freelance lifestyle journalist, and cookbook author. "Building the Future," "Fishing from the Roof of the House," and "Skiing Barefoot Over the Wrecks" first appeared in *The Treasures That Prevail* and are used by permission of Whitepoint Press LLC.

Steven Knepper teaches literature and writing at Virginia Military Institute. His poems have appeared in journals such as *Pembroke Magazine*, *SLANT*, and *Floyd County Moonshine*. "Breech" first appeared in *Glass*. "Carousel Man" was first published in *The Journal of American Poetry*. "Heartwood" appears here for the first time.

Judy Kronenfeld, Riverside, California, has published four full-length collections of poetry and two chapbooks. Her most recent book of poetry is *Bird Flying through the Banquet* (FutureCycle Press, 2017). Her poems have appeared widely in print and online journals, and in twenty anthologies. She more occasionally publishes short fiction and creative nonfiction. Judy is also the author of a critical study, *King Lear and the Naked Truth* (Duke University Press, 1998). She is Lecturer Emerita, Creative Writing Department, University of California, Riverside, and an Associate Editor of the online poetry journal, *Poemeleon*. "Cool Santa Anas" was first published in *Stirring*, reprinted in *Shimmer* (WordTech Editions, 2012); "Time Zone" first published in *The Pedestal*, reprinted in *Shimmer*; and "The Imaginary Doctors" first published in *Poetry International*; reprinted in *Light Lowering in Diminished Sevenths*, 2nd edition (Antrim House, 2012).

Hiram Larew's poems have appeared most recently in such places as *vox poetica*, *Amsterdam Quarterly*, *Seminary Ridge Review*, and in his third collection, *Utmost* (I. Giraffe Press, 2016). From Upper Marlboro, Maryland, he is a member of the Folger Shakespeare Library's Poetry Board and his poetry papers are held in the Washington Writers Archive Collection at the George Washington University's Gelman Library. "Boy Howdy" first appeared in *Broadkill Review*; "Ten Years" first appeared in *Digges' Choice*; and "Better Seeds" first appeared in *RUBY*.

Dawn Leas lives in Kingston, Pennsylvania, and is the author of a full-length collection, *Take Something When You Go* (Winter Goose Publishing, 2016), and a chapbook, *I Know When to Keep Quiet* (Finishing Line Press, 2010). In past lives she has been a copywriter, freelancer, and English teacher. She received an M.F.A. in Creative Writing from Wilkes University where she is now the assistant to the president. "Impressions" was first published in *Word Fountain*. "Good Girls" and "Gypsy" appear here for the first time.

From Englewood, New Jersey, **Annmarie Lockhart** is editor and publisher of unbound CONTENT, as well as the daily poetry venue *vox* *poetica*. Her work appears in numerous places, including *Scratching Against the Fabric* (unbound CONTENT, 2015). "Eternal June," "To Sir Bob, with Love," and "A Breach of Etiquette" appear here for the first time.

Andrew Manyika is an award-winning writer and performer based in Harare, Zimbabwe. He has previously been published in the South African anthology, *Home Is Where The Mic Is* (Botsotso Publishing, 2015), and in 2016 his debut one-man show, *Andrew Manyika's: Love & Laughter*, opened to critical acclaim in Zimbabwe. 2017 saw his international career begin to flourish with performances in America at the Bridgewater International Poetry Festival, as well as the Backdoor Comedy Club in Dallas, Texas, and the Furious Flower Poetry Centre in Virginia, USA. "Refuse," "Ode to Bacon," "Space-Time," and "Wondering Why While Wandering Where" appear in print here for the first time.

John J. McKenna is a New York-born, Princeton-based writer, whose efforts range from poetry and longer prose to academic studies. John is a grateful member of the New Hope Beat Poets Society (New Hope, Pennsylvania). John's inspiration—beyond the visits of myriad Muses—flows from Rumi, Emerson, and Whitman through Ginsberg, Jack K., and Bukowski to current torchbearers—flamethrowers—hell raisers like Kim Addonizio. John believes in wine, women and song. In addition to John's first collection of poetry *Sessions* (Red Dashboard, 2016), his poetry has appeared in *The River Poets Journal* and *vox poetica*. "A cup of coffee, a cigarette and an attempt to read the day's newspaper," "On Russian Hill," and "Who's That with the Horn" all first appeared in *Sessions*.

Seth Michelson teaches the poetry of the Americas at Washington and Lee University. He is the author of five collections of poetry, most recently *Swimming Through Fire* (Press 53, 2017). He also has translated six books of poetry, most recently rendering *El canto rojo* (Sediento Ediciones, 2013), by the Uruguayan poet Melisa Machado, as *The Red Song* (Action Books, 2017). "Papa's War Song" and "Sexual Violence" first appeared in *Swimming Through Fire*. His introduction to this volume appears here for the first time.

John Most lives in Crozet, Virginia. His latest book of poems is *What Thoughts* (Authorspress, 2015). "A Very Tall Building," "Airplanes," and "Stargazing on Fire Mountain" appear here for the first time.

Sarah Murphy is a Connecticut-born, Virginia-raised poet. She is also a photographer, activist, film-maker, designer, and artist. "Life/Force" appears here for the first time.

Susan Notar is a poet living in Northern Virginia. Her work has appeared in a number of publications including *NoVA Bards*, *Joys of the Table, An Anthology of Culinary Verse*, *Penumbra*, and *American Literary.* She is a member of the Poetry Society of Virginia, from which she has won awards, and the Arlington Writer's Group. In the winter of 2017, she participated in the Northern Virginia Poet/Painter/Musician Collaborative. She works at the U.S. State Department on human rights in the Middle East. "Hands with Grapes" and "Equinox" first appeared in *Northern Virginia Bards.* "Semana Santa" appears here for the first time.

Laura Sloan Patterson is an English professor at Seton Hill University in Greensburg, Pennsylvania. Her poetry has appeared in *Lines + Stars*, *Spry*, *Pittsburgh Poetry Review*, and several other journals. She was a finalist for the 2016 James Applewhite Poetry Prize. "Pomegranate" first appeared in *Spry* and "Predawn Eastern Sky" was first published in *Lines + Stars.*

George Perreault is from Reno, Nevada, and his most recent collection of poetry is *Bodark County*, featuring poems in the voices of characters living on the Llano Estacado. He has received a fellowship from the Nevada Arts Council and an award from the Washington Poets Association, was a finalist for the Backwaters Prize, and has served as a visiting writer in New Mexico, Montana, and Utah. His poems have been nominated for the Pushcart Prize and selected for nine anthologies and dozens of magazines; recent work can be found in *The American Journal of Poetry*, *High Desert Journal*, *Weber – The Contemporary West*, *San Pedro River Review*, and *Gravel.* "Once Upon," "The Black Road North," and "The Color Wheel" appear here for the first time.

Sara M. Robinson, award-winning poet, founder of the Lonesome Mountain Pros(e) Writers' Workshop, and Instructor of a course on Contemporary American Poets at UVA-OLLI, is poetry columnist for *Southern Writers Magazine* and poetry editor for *Virginia Literary Journal.* In addition to publication in various anthologies and journals, she is author of five books, most recently *Stones for Words* (Cedar

Creek, 2014) and *Sometimes the Little Town* (Cedar Creek, 2016). "Writing Poetry With Putin" first appeared at *vox poetica*. "A Poem Written as Scars" appears here for the first time.

Albert Russo has published worldwide over 85 books of poetry, fiction and photography, in English and in French, most recently *The Gosh Zapinette!* Series (cyberwit.net [India], 2016) and *African Quatuor* (The Aleph [Sweden], 2014). He is the recipient of many awards: The American Society of Writers Fiction Award, The British Diversity Short Story Award, several New York Poetry Forum Awards, Prix Colette, Prix de la Liberté, Prix UNICEF 2013, among others. His work has been broadcast on the BBC and translated into a dozen languages. He now lives in Tel Aviv, Israel, after having resided on three other continents—Africa (Central, Eastern and Southern Africa), America (NYC) and Europe (Milan, Brussels, and Paris). "The Rose City of Petra," "A Young Man of Our Times," and "Invitation to Sing in French" appear here for the first time.

Amie Sharp lives in Colorado Springs, Colorado. Her work has appeared in *Atticus Review*, the *Bellevue Literary Review*, and *Tar River Poetry*, among others, and has been nominated for a Pushcart Prize and Best of the Net. "Diabetes" originally appeared in *Rearrange*. "The Minister's Last Morning" was first published in *Grey Sparrow Journal*. "My Secret Poems" first appeared in *Pisgah Review*.

A rhetoric and composition instructor at Virginia Military Institute and Blue Ridge Community College, **Mattie Quesenberry Smith** recently published poems in *Dark Matter: A Journal of Speculative Writing*, *Thirty Days: Best of the 30/30 Poetry Project* (Tupelo Press), and *Red Earth Review*. "Terror Is the Placebo" and "Out of the Wind You All but Loved" appear here for the first time.

A native of Germany, **Geraldine Poppke Suter** holds a BA in English, and Master of Arts degrees in English and German. She is completing her dissertation on Alfred Döblin's dramatic texts, a project for which she has translated portions of the plays into English. She has also translated letters, historical and medical documents, and library materials. She interprets between English and German for her family members on both sides of the Atlantic Ocean. "Dem Schlaf," a translation of Stan Galloway's poem "To Sleep," is her first poetic translation, and appears in print here for the first time.

For 26 years, **William Sypher** lived and worked as an English professor in five Middle Eastern countries: Iran, Saudi Arabia, Bahrain, Qatar, and Oman. Living in the desert under an all too frequently featureless sky inspired him to turn within and to study and write about life at ground level. He now lives in Barboursville, Virginia. "Let's Pretend" first appeared in *Skyline 2017*. "Golden Dragon Babies" and "The Mosque That Built Itself" appear here for the first time.

Trevor Tingle spent his early youth hitchhiking and hopping trains, his later youth sailing tall ships, and began adult life as a Mississippi River crew boat captain. He currently works as a stay-at-home father in Richmond, Virginia. He has been or will be published by *Phantom Drift*, *Fly Catcher*, and *Slipstream* among others. "Fracturing Light on Water" first appeared in *A Narrow Fellow*; and "North Wind, Lunenburg Bound" is printed here for the first time.

Michael Waterson grew up in Pittsburgh, Pennsylvania, and has lived in California for more than forty years. He received a BA and an MFA in Creative Writing from San Francisco State University and Mills College, respectively. A retired journalist, his poetry has won several awards and has appeared in numerous literary publications and websites. He is Poet Laureate Emeritus of the Napa Valley. "Elvis in Hell" was awarded first prize in the Jessamyn West Creative Writing Contest Anthology, 2005. "Steel Season" won first prize in the Valley Writer Contest, 1992, published in the *Daily Republic* newspaper, Fairfield, California.

Maryann Wolfe lives in Harrisonburg, Virginia, and teaches Creative Writing and Food Writing at Bridgewater College. She has had work published in *Earth's Daughters* and received awards from the Virginia Poetry Society. "Coffee Break" appears here for the first time.

Nicole Yurcaba, Mathias, West Virginia, teaches at Bridgewater College in Bridgewater, Virginia, and is assistant director for the Bridgewater International Poetry Festival. Her most recent chapbook is *Hollow Bottles* (Red Dashboard, 2016). "The Pale Goth Buys Blank Journals at Target" and "The Pale Goth Fastens Her Dress" were first printed in *GNU Journal*. "A Peter Murphy Kind of Night" appears here for the first time.

Ed Zahniser lives in Shepherdstown, West Virginia. His poetry appears in five chapbooks, 10 anthologies, and five books, including *Mall-hopping* *with the Great I AM* (Somondoco Press, 2006) and *At the End of the Self-help Rope* (Scarith Press, 2016). He has edited poetry for the *Good News Paper*, *Wilderness*, and *Antietam Review* and recorded for "The Poet and the Poem" Library of Congress archive. He edited and wrote many prose books on parks, wilderness, and U.S. conservation history as senior editor and writer for the National Park Service Publications Group. "First Thing" was originally published in *Praxilla*. "November Picnic at Kohl's Department Store" and "Why We Should Not Brag About Our Emotional Depth" appear here for the first time.

Selected Titles Published by Unbound Content

Tongues in Trees
The Pomegranate Papers
This is how honey runs
Wednesday
By Cassie Premo Steele

Mothers Ought to Utter Only Niceties
A Bank Robber's Bad Luck With His Ex-Girlfriend
By KJ Hannah Greenberg

Just Married
By Stan Galloway

Backwoods and Back Words
By Nicole Yurcaba

Assumption
Earthmover
By Jim Davis

Before the Great Troubling
Our Locust Years
By Corey Mesler

Elegy
By Raphaela Willington

Inspiration 2 Smile
By Nate Spears

In New Jersey
By Julie Ellinger Hunt

Painting Czeslawa Kwoka: Honoring Children of the Holocaust
By Theresa Senato Edwards and Lori Schreiner

Saltian
By Alice Shapiro

www.ingramcontent.com/pod-product-compliance
Lightning Source LLC
Chambersburg PA
CBHW071339090426
42738CB00012B/2938
* 9 7 8 1 9 3 6 3 7 3 5 8 1 *